Shorter Dictionary of Catch Phrases

The Partridge Collection

A Dictionary of Slang and Unconventional English
Eric Partridge
Edited by Paul Beale
Eighth Edition
ISBN 0–415–06568–2 (hb)

A Concise Dictionary of Slang and Unconventional English
Edited by Paul Beale
Based on the work of Eric Partridge
ISBN 0–415–06352–3 (pb)

Origins: An Etymological Dictionary of Modern English
Eric Partridge
Fourth Edition
ISBN 0–415–05077–4 (hb)

A Dictionary of Catch Phrases
Eric Partridge
Edited by Paul Beale
Second Edition
ISBN 0–415–05916–X (pb)

A Dictionary of Clichés
Eric Partridge
Fifth Edition
ISBN 0–415–06555–0 (pb)

Shakespeare's Bawdy
Eric Partridge
Third Edition
ISBN 0–415–05076–6 (pb)

Shorter Slang Dictionary
Rosalind Fergusson
From the work of Eric Partridge & Paul Beale
ISBN 0–415–08866–6 (pb)

You Have a Point There
Eric Partridge
ISBN 0–415–05075–8 (pb)

Shorter Dictionary of Catch Phrases

Rosalind Fergusson

From the work of
Eric Partridge and Paul Beale

London and New York

First published 1994
by Routledge
11 New Fetter Lane, London EC4P 4EE

Simultaneously published in the USA and Canada
by Routledge
29 West 35th Street, New York, NY 10001

© Routledge 1994

Typeset in Baskerville by the EPPP Group at Routledge
Printed and bound in Great Britain by TJ Press (Padstow) Ltd, Cornwall
Printed on acid-free paper

British Library Cataloguing in Publication Data
A catalogue record for this book is available from the British Library

Library of Congress Cataloging in Publication Data
A catalog record for this book is available from the Library of Congress

ISBN 0–415–10051–8

101075025

Foreword

This volume has been derived from the magisterial work of Eric Partridge and his collaborator and successor Paul Beale. Most of the entries have been adapted from material in the second edition (1985) of the classic *A Dictionary of Catch Phrases*, although articles have also been specially written for items that came into currency in the 1990s.

The focus throughout is on expressions that are in current daily use, and familiar throughout most parts of the English-speaking world. Items originating in Britain, the United States, Canada, Australia and New Zealand are all to be found within these covers.

We at Routledge are proud to publish this companion volume to the *Shorter Dictionary of Slang* (1993) as a tribute to Eric Partridge on the occasion of the centenary of his birth on 6 February 1894.

A

Abyssinia! a pun on 'I'll be seeing you!'. It probably predates the Abyssinian War of 1935–6 and may have arisen from the British campaign of 1899 against the 'Mad Mullah' or from General Napier's expedition of 1868. Similar puns include *Alaska* (= I'll ask her) and *Jamaica* (= did you make her).

accidentally on purpose apparently accidental, but really – and often maliciously – on purpose. The phrase has been used in the UK since around 1880 and in the USA since around 1885.

accidents will happen in the best-regulated families see **it happens in the best-regulated** (or **best of**) **families**.

according to plan used ironically for anything, however trivial, that does not go according to plan. In World War I communiqués the phrase was a frequent excuse for failure, e.g. an enforced retreat.

act to follow, a hard (or **tough**) refers to any outstanding performance or especially able person. It often carries the implication 'don't blame me if I fail'. The phrase originated, probably before 1920, in vaudeville, referring to an outstandingly successful act that might well cast a shadow over the following act.

act your age! don't be childish!; act like an adult and use your intelligence! Adopted from the USA around 1920. See also **be your age!**; **grow up!**

against my religion, it's see **it's against my religion**.

age before beauty used jocularly when giving precedence or priority to an older person, as on entering a room. The phrase originated in the late 19th century. There are a number of standard retorts, such as 'no, dust before the broom' and the classic 'pearls before swine', attributed to the US writer Dorothy Parker.

age of miracles is not past, the a delighted exclamation of surprise at a gratifyingly unexpected occurrence. In its original opposite form *the age of miracles is past*, the phrase was used contentiously by freethinkers during the 18th century, challengingly by agnostics during the 19th century and by most cynics and sceptics in the 20th century.

aha, me proud beauty! means 'now I've got you where I want you!'

The phrase originated in melodrama, traditionally addressed by the villain to a hapless and helpless female, in the late 19th century. Since the 1920s or earlier it has been chiefly used for comic effect.

ain't nobody here but us chickens!(, there)   used on occasions when unexpectedly few people are present, or as a warning that others had better stay away. The phrase originated in the USA in the late 19th century and was adopted in the UK around 1950. It was based on a story about a chicken-thief surprised by the owner, who calls 'Anybody there?' and is greeted by this reply. Several variations of this story exist, and the line subsequently became the chorus of a popular song. The phrase was revived in the 1980s in the UK television comedy series, *Nightingales.*

ain't you got no homes to go to?   see **time, gentlemen, please . . ..**

Alaska   see **Abyssinia!**

alive and well and living in . . .   a slogan or response, as in *God is alive and well and living in Hampstead; 'I haven't seen old Jack for years – he must be dead by now.' 'No, he's alive and well and living in Manchester.'* The phrase may date back to the early 20th century. In the late 1960s it was used in the title of the show *Jacques Brel is alive and well and living in Paris.*

all ashore that's (or **as is**) **going ashore!**   used e.g. by the driver of a car hastening the passengers, or rather the passengers' friends, who are taking too long to say goodbye. In its original nautical context the phrase probably dates back to the days of the earliest scheduled passenger liners.

all bitter and twisted   applied to somebody who is badly warped by life's mishaps, e.g. a man psychologically scarred by wartime experiences. The phrase is sometimes used compassionately, but more often unthinkingly and insensitively.

all chiefs and no Indians   applied to any concern or establishment that seems to be management-heavy. Since around 1950. The phrase probably originated in the USA, together with the variant *too many chiefs and not enough Indians.*

all clever stuff   see **it's all clever stuff, y'know.**

all contributions gratefully received(, however small)   a request for or response to the donation of anything, not necessarily money, as in *'I've only got half a cheese sandwich left, but you're welcome to that if you want it.' 'All contributions gratefully received – thanks!'* Since around 1925.

all day!   said in response to such questions as 'It's Wednesday (or the 25th) today, isn't it?' The phrase is also added to the reply to such questions as 'What day is it today?' or 'What's the date?', as in *it's*

Friday, all day! Since around 1890 or earlier.

all done with mirrors(**, it's**)   applied to anything that seems very clever or extremely ingenious. Since the late 19th century. The phrase occurs in Noël Coward's *Private Lives* (1930): 'Death's very laughable, such a cunning little mystery. All done with mirrors.' It originally referred to the mirrors used in stage illusions and conjuring tricks, such as Pepper's Ghost. Variants include *all done with pieces of string*, a possible allusion to the contraptions designed by W. Heath Robinson, and (in US usage) *all done with a simple twist of the wrist.*

all dressed up and no place (or **nowhere**) **to go**   originated in the song 'When You're All Dressed Up and Have No Place to Go', popularized around 1914–15 by the US comedian Raymond Hitchcock.

all dressed up like a Christmas tree   wearing one's best clothes; flashily dressed or overdressed. Since the late 19th century. There are numerous variants of the phrase, including *all dressed up like a pox-doctor's clerk* (since around 1870) and *(all) dressed* (or *done*) *up like a dog's dinner* (since around 1925). The variant *all dressed up like a ham bone*, dating from around 1850 but virtually obsolete by 1970, probably referred to the paper frill used to decorate a joint of ham on the bone when it was brought to table.

all good clean fun   see **it's all good clean fun**

all hands on deck!   a rallying call for assistance, as in *come on, all hands on deck – let's get this mess cleared up!* Of nautical origin.

all human life is there!   popularized as an advertising slogan for the *News of the World* in the late 1950s. The phrase originated in Henry James's *Madonna of the Future* (1879): 'Cats and monkeys – monkeys and cats – all human life is there!'

all I know is what I read in the papers   popularized by the US actor and humorist Will Rogers in the 1920s. The phrase has a number of possible interpretations or implications: 'it must be true, I read it in the newspaper'; 'it's not my opinion, I read it in the newspaper'; 'I have no other source of information'; 'I'm just an average citizen, not a political analyst'; 'I'm not particularly well-read'; etc.

all mouth and trousers   applied to a loud-mouthed person who makes empty boasts, threats, etc., as in *take no notice of him: he's all mouth and trousers*. Since the mid-20th century; possibly a euphemistic variant of the earlier phrase *all prick and breeches*. See also **all piss and wind**.

all my eye and Betty Martin!   that is utter nonsense! Since the 18th century. The identity of Betty Martin has been the subject of much discussion. Partridge suspects that she was a 'character' of the lusty London of the 1770s, and that no record of her exists other than in this catch phrase. More erudite but less probable explanations suggest that the phrase is a corruption of the invocation *O mihi, beate Martine* (to St Martin of Tours) or *O mihi, Britomartis* (to the tutelary goddess of Crete).

all my own work   used jocularly or ironically, especially in an ironically self-deprecatory manner. From around 1920. The phrase probably originated in the drawings and paintings displayed by pavement artists.

all over bar the shouting(, it's)   it is (virtually) finished or decided; there is only the official announcement to come. Since 1842 or earlier. The word *but* (or *except*) is sometimes substituted for *bar*, especially in US usage and in early British usage.

all over the place like a mad woman's shit   describes a state of complete untidiness or confusion. Chiefly used in Australia in the later 20th century. The word *knitting* (or *custard*) is sometimes politely substituted for *shit.*

all part of life's rich pattern(, it's)   an ironically resigned, yet far from submissive, reflection upon the vicissitudes of life. The phrase may have originated as *it's all part of life's rich pageant,* used by the British writer and entertainer Arthur Marshall in the monologue 'The Games Mistress' (1937) and further popularized by Peter Sellers as Inspector Clouseau in the film *A Shot in the Dark* (1964). Other variants substitute *tapestry* or *fabric* for *pattern.*

all part of the service   see **it's all** (or **just**) **part of the service**.

all piss and wind   applied contemptuously to somebody who is given to much talk (especially boasting) and little, if any, performance. The phrase originated in the 18th-century simile *like the barber's cat, all wind and piss,* which has the 20th-century variants *all wind* (or *crumbs*) *and piss like the bottom of a baby's pram* and *all wind and no piss* (or *water*), meaning 'all talk and no action'. See also **all mouth and trousers.**

all present and correct!   all in order. From the phrase used by a sergeant-major reporting on a parade to the officer in charge.

all right for some!(, it's)   some people have all the luck! An expression of (often jocular) disgruntlement. 20th century.

all right on the night   see **it'll be all right on the night**.

all-singing, all-dancing   applied to computers and other machines or systems that have the full range of additions, elaborations, modifications, etc. (These additions are often referred to as *bells and whistles.*) Since around 1970.

all systems go   a statement of preparedness for an endeavour, as in *it's all systems go here.* The phrase was popularized worldwide in the late 1960s and early 1970s, when it was used as a statement of readiness for launching a spacecraft.

although (or **though**) **I says it as shouldn't** appended to a remark. The phrase dates back at least to the early 17th century, being used in Beaumont and Fletcher's *Wit at Several Weapons*: 'Though I say it that should not say it.' The more grammatical form *although I say it who* (or *that*) *shouldn't* is a less frequent variant in modern usage.

always read the small print in business and legal matters, make absolutely sure you know what you're letting yourself in for. Since around 1955. The phrase may be used figuratively or literally, referring to print so small that you risk severe eyestrain if you read it carefully, and bankruptcy if you don't.

and a merry Christmas to you too! thank you for nothing! Addressed ironically to somebody who has deliberately or inadvertently done something annoying or unhelpful. Since around 1930. The phrase is also used in the sense of 'the same to you with knobs on!' (see **same to you . . .**).

and all that and all such things. The phrase was in Standard English before 1929, when Robert Graves's *Goodbye to All That* was published; it became a catch phrase after the publication of W. C. Sellar and R. J. Yeatman's comic history of England, *1066 and All That*, in 1930.

and don't you forget it! an admonitory intensifier, as in *I'm the boss around here, and don't you forget it!* (The word *it* usually refers to something that is unpleasant and quite unforgettable.) Adopted from the USA around 1890.

and how! intensifies or indicates emphatic agreement with what has just been said. Used in the USA from around 1925; adopted in the UK during the 1930s. Possibly a translation of the phrase *e come!* used by the large Italian population of the USA.

and I don't mean maybe adds force or emphasis to what has gone before. The phrase has been used in the USA since around 1920, popularized by the song that begins 'Yes, sir, that's my baby, / No, sir, don't mean maybe', by Walter Donaldson and Gus Kahn.

and like it! used in response to or anticipation of a complaint about something unwanted or unpleasant, as in *the flight is fully booked: you'll have to take the ferry and like it!* 'She wants smoked salmon in her sandwiches.' 'Too bad – she can have fish paste and like it!' The phrase may have originated in the armed forces during World War I, with reference to an awkward or unwanted job.

and no mistake without any doubt; an expression of affirmation, as in *this is an embarrassing situation and no mistake.* From around 1810.

and now for something completely different a catch phrase of the television series *Monty Python's Flying Circus* (first broadcast in 1969 in the UK), satirizing the use of such phrases in broadcasting to link two dissimilar programmes, magazine items, news items, etc. The phrase was also used as the title of the first Monty Python film (1971).

and so to bed a quotation from Samuel Pepys's *Diary* of 1660 that became a catch phrase in the 19th century. The phrase was further popularized in 1926 by James Bernard Fagan's comedy *And So to Bed*, subtitled 'An Adventure with Pepys'.

and so we say farewell a phrase originally used at the end of B-grade film travelogues. It is satirically repeated (usually in a mock-American accent) in parodies of such films, notably Peter Sellers' skit that ends 'and so we say "farewell" to Bal-ham, gateway to the South!', a recording of which helped to popularize the phrase in the late 1950s.

and that ain't hay! that's a lot of money!, as in *they offered him $5000, and that ain't hay!* Used in the USA since the 1940s or earlier.

and that's flat! used to emphasize a preceding remark, especially a refusal or final decision, as in *I'm not coming with you, and that's flat!* British usage of the phrase is long established – it occurs as early as Shakespeare.

and that's your lot! that's all you're going to receive, so don't expect any more! Since around 1920.

and the band played on things went on as usual. From the refrain of the song 'The Band Played On', with lyrics by John F. Palmer, published in New York in 1895.

and the rest! said with trenchant sarcasm, in response to a gross understatement or the omission of something significant, as in *'It'll only cost you a tenner.' 'And the rest!'* Since around 1860.

and then some and even more, as in *we need to work 24 hours a day and then some*. The phrase entered British usage from the USA around 1913, but it may have originated in the Scottish phrase *and some*, which dates back to the 18th century or earlier.

and very nice too! see **very nice too!**

angle of dangle is inversely proportional to the heat of the meat, the a catch phrase among better-educated National Servicemen of the 1950s, axiomatic for the degree of male sexual excitement.

another day, another dollar said at the end of a hard working day (referring to the day that has just passed) or at the end of a bad day (referring to a hoped-for better day tomorrow). Used in the USA from around 1910 and in the UK since the late 1940s. The US poet Ogden Nash used the phrase punningly in his verse 'A Man Can Complain, Can't He' (A Lament for Those Who Think Old): 'I'm old too soon, yet young too long; / Could Swift himself have planned it droller? / *Timor vitae conturbat me,* / Another day, another dolor.'

another fine mess you've gotten me into! (, here's) a catch phrase of the Laurel and Hardy films, one of which bore the title *Another Fine Mess.* The phrase was Oliver Hardy's standing reproach to his duller-witted partner Stan Laurel. A catch phrase of the 1930s and 1940s, it came back into general use when the films were shown on television. In British usage *gotten* is sometimes replaced by *got.*

answer is a lemon, the a derisive non-reply to a query, or a refusal of a request. The phrase originated in the USA, where one of the slang senses of *lemon* is 'a sharp verbal thrust, criticism, or retort', and was adopted in the UK around 1919. Other explanations of the origin of the phrase refer to the sourness or acidity of a lemon, the low-scoring lemons of a fruit machine, or the slang use of the word with reference to anything defective or undesirable.

answer is in the plural and they bounce, the a jocularly polite way of saying 'balls!', meaning 'nonsense!'. The phrase is often attributed to the British architect Sir Edwin Lutyens, who is said to have used it before a Royal Commission, but he may have been quoting an already established catch phrase (if, in fact, he ever used the phrase at all).

any colour you like, so long as it's black applied to any situation of limited choice or Hobson's choice, in which you can take it or leave it. The phrase is based on a slogan of the Ford Motor Company, referring to the (lack of) colour options for the Model T; it became a catch phrase in the UK in the late 1940s.

any complaints? a way of opening a conversation when there's nothing else to say. The question was originally asked by the orderly officer doing his meal-time rounds of the other ranks' dining-hall; as a catch phrase it is chiefly used by former members of the armed forces. Since World War II.

any joy? have you had (or did you have) any luck? The phrase has been used in the USA since around 1930 and in the UK since the 1940s or earlier. Similarly, the phrase *no joy* is used to report a lack of success or satisfaction.

any more for any more? does anybody (else) want a second helping?; does anybody else want to join in?; etc. Since World War I.

anyone for tennis? used to initiate a conversation. Since around 1910. The phrase is stereotypical of social comedies featuring the leisured classes, in which a young man or woman enters through the French windows of a country house brandishing a tennis racket. Variants include *tennis, anyone?* and *who's for tennis?* None of these phrases has been found in the text of an actual play, although there are several near misses, one of the earliest and closest occurring in George Bernard Shaw's *Misalliance* (1914): 'Anybody on for a game of tennis?'

anyone's bet(, it's or **that's)** nobody can say for certain. Since the early 1970s.

anything for a laugh a cliché that may be regarded as a catch phrase when it is used with the implication of going too far in a situation where laughter is inappropriate, as in *I wouldn't risk it but you know him – he'll do anything for a laugh.* Since around 1945.

anything goes! anything is permissible; do as you please. Used in the USA from around 1930, the phrase was popularized by the Cole Porter song and musical comedy *Anything Goes* (1934), and was soon adopted in the UK.

anything that *can* **go wrong** *will* **go wrong** a summary of Murphy's law, also known (in the UK since around 1970) as Sod's law. This principle is also expressed in the form *if anything can go wrong, it will,* sometimes with the rider *and if it can't go wrong, it might.* Possibly of US origin, since around 1950. The best-known illustration of the law is that bread always falls on its buttered side, a phenomenon observed as early as the 19th century, when Tom Hood the Younger wrote: 'I never nursed a dear gazelle, / To glad me with its dappled hide, / But when it came to know me well / It fell upon the buttered side' (a parody of Thomas Moore's famous quatrain from *Lalla Rookh*). This parody was echoed in 1884 in James Payn's verse: 'I never had a piece of toast / Particularly long and wide / But fell upon the sanded floor / And always on the buttered side.'

apples, she's (or **she'll be**) everything is (or will be) all right. Used in Australia since around 1950. The use of the word *apples* in this context may be derived from the phrase *apple-pie order* or the phrase *apples and spice* (Australian rhyming slang for 'nice'). See also **she's right!**

are there any more at home like you? addressed to an attractive girl or young woman. 20th century. From the musical comedy *Floradora* (first performed in 1900), which contained the song 'Tell me, pretty maiden, are there any more at home like you?'

are we downhearted? a cry of encouragement, to which the usual answer is 'no!' (but sometimes, jocularly, 'yes!'). The phrase is political in origin (from around 1906) and did not achieve the status of a true catch phrase until World War I.

are you a man or a mouse? addressed to a timorous person. Adopted from the USA around 1945. There are a number of standard ripostes, such as 'squeak, squeak!' and 'a man: my wife's frightened of mice'.

are you kidding? are you joking?; surely you're not serious? Since
   around 1945, probably of US origin. See also **you're joking!**
are you sitting comfortably? (Then I'll begin) the introductory line
   of the children's radio programme *Listen with Mother*, used by Julia
   Lang at the beginning of the first broadcast (in January 1950 in the
   UK) and retained by popular demand. It became a catch phrase of
   the 1950s–60s and is still heard from time to time.
are you trying to tell me something? a response to a vague or indirect
   hint (or, ironically, to a clear and unambiguous hint). Probably of
   US origin; used in the UK since around 1965. See also **I guess you're
   trying to tell me something**.
are you with me? do you understand?; do you follow me? Since
   around 1920. In modern usage the phrase is often shortened to *with
   me?*; the corresponding phrase *with you!* means 'I understand'. An
   advertising campaign of the 1970s by the Woolwich Building Society
   gave rise to the jocular reply *no, I'm with the Woolwich*, now rather
   dated.
aren't we all? suggests that an attribute, condition, etc., is common to
   all or most people, as in *'I'm an abject coward.' 'Aren't we all?'* Since
   around 1918 or earlier. Variants for use in other contexts include
   don't we all? and *doesn't everyone?*
aren't you (or **I**) **the lucky one!** see **lucky one!, aren't you** (or **I**) **the**.
aren't you the one! an expression of quizzical or rueful admiration.
   Used in the USA since around 1942 and in the UK in the later 20th
   century. See also **you are a one!**
arm and a leg, an refers to an exorbitant price or charge, as in *it'll cost
   you an arm and a leg*. Adopted from the USA, where the phrase has
   been in general use since the 1940s or earlier. A cartoon on the cover
   of *Time Out* in 1982 showed a would-be traveller on the London
   Underground, where the fares had just been raised enormously,
   offering his sawn-off arm and leg at the ticket window.
as camp as a row of tents see **camp as a row of tents**.
as clear as mud see **clear as mud**.
as happy (or **lucky**) **as a bastard on Father's Day** see **happy as a bastard on Father's Day**.
as happy as a pig in shit see **happy as a pig in shit**.
as I live and breathe indicates confidence, assurance or certainty;
   often used to emphasize (the truth of) an assertion, or as an
   exclamation of surprise, as in *she's guilty, as I live and breathe*, *Mr
   Frobisher, as I live and breathe!* Variants of the phrase date from around
   1645.
as I used to was a jocular variant of 'as I used to be', as in *I'm not so fit*

as I used to was. 20th century.

as if I cared!　a catch phrase of the character Sam Fairfechan (played by Hugh Morton) in the radio series *ITMA* (*It's That Man Again*), first broadcast in 1939 in the UK. The phrase was usually preceded by the polite inquiry 'Good morning, how are you today?'

as large as life and twice as natural　see **large as life and twice as natural.**

as much chance as a snowball in hell　see **snowball's chance in hell, a**

as nutty as a fruitcake　see **nutty as a fruitcake.**

as old as my tongue and a little older than my teeth　see **old as my tongue and a little older than my teeth.**

as queer as Dick's hatband　see **queer as Dick's hatband.**

as soft as shit and twice as nasty　see **soft as shit and twice as nasty, as.**

as the actress said to the bishop　a sexual innuendo added to an innocent remark, creating a double entendre, as in *it's too stiff for me to manage it, as the actress said to the bishop.* Where appropriate, the variant *as the bishop said to the actress* is used instead, as in *I can't keep this up for long, as the bishop said to the actress.* The phrase probably dates back to Edwardian times.

as thick as two short planks　see **thick as two short planks.**

ask a silly question and you'll get a silly answer　said in response to such a question or answer, or as a truculent justification for having given a silly answer to a (debatably) silly question; sometimes shortened to *ask a silly question!* Since the late or mid-19th century. The phrase may have evolved from the proverb *ask no questions and you'll be told no lies.*

ass in a sling, have (or **get**) **(one's)**　to be in (or get into) deep trouble or difficulties, as in *don't get your ass in a sling.* Used in the USA since the 1930s or earlier and in the UK in the later 20th century.

at least she won't die wondering　see **she'll die wondering.**

attaboy!　an exclamation of warm approval or great admiration, e.g. for something exceptionally well done. Adopted from the USA around 1918. This one-word catch phrase is a contraction of *that's the boy!* The feminine form *attagirl!* is less frequent. See also **that's my boy!**

aw shucks!　an expression of embarrassment; used in jocular imitation of a US or Canadian yokel. Since around 1910. The word *shucks* is probably a euphemism for *shit.*

B

back to square one let's start again from the very beginning, often through reluctant necessity; also used by those who find themselves back at the very beginning, having made no net progress. The origin of the phrase (in January 1927) is said to be the former BBC method of dividing the football pitch into squares for radio commentary purposes. However, the commentators themselves may have taken the phrase from such games as snakes and ladders, where an unlucky throw of the dice may take a player back to the first square of the board, or from the game of hopscotch, in which a grid of squares similar to that superimposed on the football pitch is used.

back to the drawing-board! refers to the thorough reappraisal required when a complicated project ends in failure; also used in the sense of 'let's get back to work'. The phrase probably originated in a famous cartoon of World War II, by Peter Arno of the *The New Yorker*: the cartoon depicted an aircraft exploding on the ground, watched by its designer (with a roll of technical drawings under his arm) saying 'Ah well, back to the old drawing-board.'

back to the grindstone! it's time to resume work (after a break). Often preceded by *Oh, well.* The phrase probably derives from the expression *keep one's* (or someone else's) *nose to the grindstone*, meaning to be, or to force someone else to be, continually engaged in hard and monotonous work, used since around 1830.

ball game, it's a different (or **whole new**) the situation has entirely changed; it's a completely different situation. The phrase has been used in the USA since the 1930s or earlier and had been adopted in the UK by the early 1970s.

balloon goes up, the refers to the moment when something of great importance takes place (or is scheduled to take place), as in *the balloon goes up at three o'clock; what time does the balloon go up?* In its original military context (from around 1915) the phrase referred to the beginning of a major offensive; in civilian usage (since around 1919) it may refer to the chief event of a show, festival, etc., or to a moment of crisis or trouble.

band played on, the see **and the band played on**.

bang, bang, you're dead! a children's catch phrase used in games of cowboys and Indians, soldiers, gangsters, etc., particularly when playing with toy or make-believe guns. It gained popularity after World War II.

bang to rights refers to 'a fair cop' – a justifiable arrest for an obvious crime, as in *to be caught bang to rights*. The phrase has been used in the underworld since before 1930 and has been in general slang usage since around 1950.

bangs like a shithouse door(, **she**) she copulates vigorously, noisily and almost ferociously. Used in Australia since around 1930. A variant of the phrase has *rat* in place of *door*.

be a devil! an (often ironic) invitation to somebody to be audacious, generous, etc., for once, as in *go on, be a devil and buy yourself a beer!* Since around 1945.

be an angel! please do me a favour, as in *be an angel and fetch my handbag for me*. Mainly used by middle-class women; since around 1930 or earlier.

be good! – and if you can't be good, be careful! jocular valedictory advice; an extension of the catch phrase *be good!* The phrase may be further extended with . . . – *and if you can't be careful, get married!* (or *buy a pram!* or (in the USA) *be sanitary!* or *name it after me!*). It probably originated as the title of a song in the early 20th century. (According to a correspondent to the *Sunday Times*, the Latin phrase *si non caste, tamen caute*, which may be rendered 'If not chastely, yet cautiously', was used by Italian priests in the 13th century.) See also **don't do anything I wouldn't do!**

be my guest! said with benevolent generosity to somebody who wishes to take something, borrow something, do something, etc., as in *'May I use your phone?' 'Be my guest!'* Since around 1950. The phrase is virtually synonymous with **feel free!** It is sometimes used in place of 'You're welcome!', acknowledging an expression of gratitude.

be seeing you! goodbye (for now). A very common non-final valediction since the mid-1940s. The phrase is short for *I'll be seeing you* (see also **Abyssinia!**), and is sometimes shortened to **see you!**

be your age! stop being childish!; act like an adult! Adopted from the USA around 1934. See also **act your age!**; **grow up!**

beats working(, **it** or **that**) a jocular comment on a job that is easy or enjoyable, or one that requires very little exertion. Used in the USA from the late 1940s and subsequently adopted in the UK.

because it's there an apparently foolish reason for an apparently foolish act; the alleged response of the mountaineer George Leigh Mallory when asked in 1923 why he wanted to climb Mount Everest.

Mallory failed in his attempt and the phrase was re-popularized by Edmund Hillary, who conquered Everest in 1953.

because the higher the fewer   a meaningless response to the meaningless question *why is a mouse when it spins?* Since around 1900. Other examples of deliberate non sequiturs include *which would you rather, or go fishing?* and the question-and-answer *'What's the difference between a chicken?' 'One of its legs is both the same.'*

been and gone and done it, I've (or **you've, he's, she's**, etc.) a jocular, sometimes rueful, emphatic form of 'I've (or you've etc.) done it', as in *well, I've been and gone and done it – we got married last week; now you've been and gone and done it, you clumsy oaf!* Late 19th–20th centuries.

bee's knees, the   the very peak of perfection; the ultimate in beauty, desirability, etc., as in *she thinks she's the bee's knees.* The phrase originated in the US around 1925 and was adopted in the UK around 1930.

believe it or not!   it may sound incredible, but it is true none the less. From 1918 the phrase was popularized in the USA (and subsequently in the UK and elsewhere) as the title of a long-running series of newspaper cartoons by Robert Leroy Ripley, depicting strange-but-true facts and phenomena.

believe you me!   used for emphasis, as in *believe you me, it was hard work!* A catch phrase of the 20th century. See also **you better believe it!**

bells and whistles   see **all singing, all dancing**.

best thing since sliced bread, the   an expression of wholehearted appreciation, often applied to a useful novelty. Used in the UK since around 1950 or earlier. The phrase may have originated in the USA, in the form *the greatest thing since sliced bread.* It is sometimes used ironically by those who despise sliced bread as inferior convenience food.

better out than in!   said by (or to) the perpetrator of a loud fart or burp. Since around 1920. An older version, *better an empty house than a bad tenant,* dates from the late 19th century and originated in an 18th-century proverb; this longer form is much rarer in modern usage.

better than a dig (or poke) in the eye with a blunt (or burnt) stick applied stoically to something that is better than nothing, or enthusiastically to something that is very much better than nothing. The phrase and most of its variants (see below) probably originated in the late 19th century. Variants include *better than a kick in the pants, better than a slap in the belly* (or *face*) *with a wet fish* (or *lettuce*), and *better than sleeping with a dead policeman.*

between a rock and a hard place   between Scylla and Charybdis; in a situation where the avoidance of one problem or danger leads to another. Since the 1950s or earlier.

Beulah, peel me a grape   see **peel me a grape**.

BFN   see **ta-ta for now!**

Big Brother is watching you!   a monitory, indeed minatory, catch phrase applied to any instance of centralized bureaucratic control or government surveillance that is considered to be a curtailment of personal freedom and privacy. The phrase originated in George Orwell's novel *Nineteen Eighty-Four* (1949), where it is a slogan of the totalitarian state of which Big Brother is the sinister omnipotent leader, 'watching' the citizens through posters and telescreens in every public and private place.

big conk: big cock   implies that a man with a large nose has a large penis. The phrase may date back to the early 19th century. The phrase *a long nose is a lady's liking* is an allusive variant. Feminine variants include *big conk: big cunt* and *large mouth: large cunt*.

big deal!   used to deflate the pretensions, enthusiasm, etc., of the person addressed, as in *'My brother's just bought a Ferrari.' 'Big deal!'* Of US origin; used in the UK since the early 1950s.

bigger they are, the harder they fall, the   indicates a fearless defiance of one's superiors. Late 19th–20th centuries. The phrase was popularized by the boxer Bob Fitzsimmons, who is said to have used it on the eve of his fight with James J. Jeffries, a much bigger man.

bird is flown, the   signifies that a prisoner has escaped from jail or that a criminal has left his hiding-place. An underworld catch phrase of the 19th century, from around 1810.

bless his (or **her** or **their**) **little cotton socks!**   a jocular benediction or benevolent expression of gratitude or admiration (especially of a baby, child, or pet animal), as in *bless their little cotton socks – they've left everything ready for us!* Since the mid-20th century. An earlier form of the phrase, *bless your little cotton socks!*, meaning 'thank you!', dates from around 1905.

blind Freddie could see that(, **even**)   any fool could see that. Used in Australia since the 1930s. Blind Freddie is glossed in G. A. Wilkes's *Dictionary of Australian Colloquialisms* as 'an imaginary figure representing the highest degree of disability or incompetence and so used as a standard of comparison'.

blinded with science   a catch phrase of Australia and New Zealand, celebrating the victory of intelligence over mere physical strength. Late 19th–20th centuries. The phrase originated in the sport of boxing around 1880, when boxers using more scientific techniques began to defeat those relying on brute force. It is believed to have given rise to the verbal idiom *to blind (sb) with science*, meaning 'to explain something in very technical language, so as to discourage (sb) from asking further questions'.

Bob's your uncle!   all will be well; it's as simple as that, as in *you just press this switch, and Bob's your uncle!* Since around 1890. According to folk etymology, the origin of the phrase lies in the open and unashamed nepotism practised by some British prime minister or other politician (such as the promotion of Balfour by his uncle Robert, Lord Salisbury). A longer variant of the phrase adds . . . *and Fanny's your aunt!*

brass-monkey weather   see **cold enough to freeze the balls off a brass monkey**.

break a leg!   good luck! Chiefly used in the theatre, where it is traditionally addressed to an actor about to go on stage on the opening night of a play or show. (According to superstition, one should not say the words 'good luck!', to avoid tempting the gods.) The phrase probably originated in the early 20th century, perhaps as a translation of the German phrase *Hals- und Beinbruch*, meaning 'break your neck and leg', also used in aviation to wish a pilot well. (Most scholars and theatrical people dismiss the anecdotal origin dating from 1865, when the actor John Wilkes Booth is alleged to have jumped onto the stage and broken his leg immediately after assassinating Abraham Lincoln.)

bright-eyed and bushy-tailed   alert and ready for anything. Possibly of US origin; since 1933 or earlier. From the apparent alertness of squirrels and other such quadrupeds.

bring on the dancing girls!   let's do something more entertaining or exciting. Used in the USA before 1920 and in the UK since the 1920s. The phrase was originally the stock impresario's cliché during Broadway musical rehearsals; it is also associated with Oriental potentates, bored with their guests, ordering the dancers to appear.

brute force and ignorance   used in connection with the repair or operation of things mechanical, especially those that are stubbornly resistant to more sophisticated techniques, as in *we got the engine running by brute force and ignorance*. The phrase is sometimes found in the extended form *brute force and bloody ignorance*.

buck stops here, the   the evasion of responsibility ends at this point; a sign that appeared on the desk of Harry S Truman at some stage during his presidency of the USA (1945–53). From the practice of passing the buck (in the idiomatic sense of the phrase) until it reaches the person who must shoulder the responsibility.

built like a brick shithouse   applied to a very well-built person, male or female. The phrase has been in use since the early 20th century.

bully for you! a mocking or ironic expression of admiration or congratulation, as in *'I won first prize.' 'Bully for you!'* The phrase has been
used in the UK since around 1870, originally as an expression of
genuine admiration or congratulation; the mocking or ironic overtones developed in the latter half of the 20th century.

business as usual carrying on with one's business, everyday activities,
etc., despite difficulty or danger; sometimes applied derisively or
censoriously to an attitude of blind complacency. A catch phrase of
World War I, it was used in a famous speech by Winston Churchill
on 9 November 1914, traditionally quoted as: 'The maxim of the
British people is "Business as usual".'

by guess and by God by guesswork rather than logical thought or
methodical reasoning, and therefore unlikely to succeed except by
divine intervention, as in *to navigate by guess and by God*. 20th century.

bye for now! see **ta-ta for now!**

C

camp as a row of tents(**, as**)   spectacularly histrionic and affected in gesture, speech, manner, movement, etc.; also applied to a blatantly homosexual male. A pun on the noun *camp* and the slang adjective *camp*, meaning 'homosexual' or 'excessively affected or theatrical in speech or manner'.

can do   yes, I can do it; yes, all right. The phrase originated in pidgin English of the mid-19th century and was widely used by the armed forces. It is also used as a question, *can do?*, meaning 'can you do it?', to which the reply may be *can do!* See also **no can do**.

can of worms   see **that's another can of worms**.

can you beat that?   can you better that (for impudence, excellence, unexpectedness, etc.)?, as in *she asked me for her old job back – can you beat that?* 20th century; probably adopted from the USA.

can't be bad!   an expression of approbation or congratulation, as in *'He gets £800 a week for about ten hours' work!' 'Can't be bad!'* The use of the phrase may have been influenced by the Beatles song 'She loves you . . . and you know that can't be bad.'

can't complain   see **fair to middling**.

can't tell shit from Shinola(**, he**)   applied to an ignorant or stupid person. The phrase was originally (before 1930) used in the US armed forces: Shinola was the brand of boot polish issued to the men.

captain is at home, the   a euphemistic reference to a woman who is having her period. The phrase originated in the mid-18th century. Perhaps from a pun on *catamenia*, menstruation. Variants include *the cardinal is come*, from the colour red associated with a cardinal, and *my* (or *her*) *country cousins have come*. The latter phrase exists in a variety of forms, with *friends, relations, aunt, grandmother*, etc., in place of *country cousins*. All these phrases were (virtually) obsolete by the mid-20th century.

carrying all before her   applied to a woman who either has a very large bust or is rather prominently pregnant. From around 1920.

casting nasturtiums   a deliberate malapropism, with *nasturtiums* in place of *aspersions*, as in *are you casting nasturtiums?* 20th century.

cat got your tongue?   see **has the cat got your tongue?**

cat in hell's chance, not a   see **not a cat in hell's chance**.

cat laugh, enough to (or **it would**) **make a**   see **enough to make a cat laugh**.

chalk it up to experience!   there's nothing to be done about it (a mistake or mishap) except learn from it. From the beginning of the 20th century or earlier. The metaphor is probably derived from the practice of chalking up debts, etc., on a slate.

chance would be a fine thing!   I only wish I had the opportunity!; you are unlikely to get the opportunity, and wouldn't know what to do with it if you did! The phrase is often used jocularly in sexual contexts, as in *'She would never be unfaithful to her husband.' 'Chance would be a fine thing!'* The phrase may date back to the 17th century; an early 20th-century example of usage occurs in William Stanley Houghton's play *Hindle Wakes* (1912).

charge like the Light Brigade(**, they**)   their prices or charges are very high. Since around 1955. A (chiefly Australian) variant of the phrase has *a wounded bull* in place of *the Light Brigade*.

cheap and cheerful   applied to something that is cheap and inferior, but nevertheless serves its purpose adequately, as in *we bought a cheap and cheerful carpet for the children's playroom*. The phrase is not as deprecating as *cheap and nasty*. Possibly since around 1950.

cheap at half the price(**, it would be**)   it's very good value, a very reasonable price; said by the seller or the buyer. The phrase dates from 1920 at the latest, perhaps from as early as 1890. It is one of those intensely idiomatic phrases that are taken for granted yet prove impossible to analyse or explain: the accepted interpretation would make more sense if *twice* were substituted for *half*. Kingsley Amis wrote in the *Observer*, 4 September 1977: 'I think it's an ironical inversion of the salesman's claim, "cheap at double the price", and means what it says, it would be cheap at half the price, i.e. it's bloody expensive.'

cheeky monkey!   usually addressed to a child or young adult, especially male. The phrase was already well established in northern English usage when it was popularized by the comedian Al Read in the 1950s.

cheer up: it may never happen   see **don't worry: it may never happen**.

chips are down, the   the situation is both grave and urgent; the time has come when a fateful decision must be made, as in *when the chips are down, ...* Of US origin, the phrase probably originated before World War I. The word *chips* refers to the counters used in poker and other games of chance.

chocks away!   get on with the job! The phrase originated in the RAF around 1920, with the literal meaning of 'remove the wooden chocks and let the planes get off the ground'. It may be applied to the first run of anything mechanical.

Christmas comes but once a year – thank God! said by those who hate to see what the profiteers have made of Christmas, or who simply dislike or resent the expense and excess involved. (The cliché *Christmas comes but once a year* is used to justify such expense or excess.) That the phrase dates from around 1945 may surprise those who feel that the commercialization of Christmas is a more recent phenomenon.

cinch, it's (or **that's**) **a** it's a certainty; that's dead easy. Used in the USA since 1900 at the latest and in the UK since the late 1930s or earlier. From the *cinch* (meaning 'girth') of a saddle, which holds it firmly and securely in position.

clear as mud(**, as**) as clear as muddy water, i.e. not at all clear; an ironic or jocular simile, as in *'Is that quite clear to you now?' 'Yes, as clear as mud!'* Since around 1820 or earlier.

clever chaps (or **devils**) **these Chinese!** see **damned clever these Chinese!**

close, but no cigar(**, it was**) a US catch phrase used chiefly in sporting contexts. Since around 1930. Perhaps from the practice of presenting a cigar to the winner of some minor competition.

close your eyes and think of England! jocular advice to a girl or young woman on her wedding night, or on any occasion when sexual intercourse is considered to be a duty rather than a pleasure; also jocularly addressed to a reluctant participant (of either sex) in any activity. A variant has *shut* in place of *close*. The phrase originated in the late 19th century, when it was probably used in more literal contexts by Britons living abroad in unpleasant conditions. See also **lie back and enjoy it!**

cloth ears, he (or **she**) **has** he (or she) does not hear, listen or respond; often applied to those who pretend not to hear what they do not wish to hear. 20th century; of Cockney origin. From caps with heavy ear-flaps.

cloud nine, on see **on cloud nine.**

cobblers! see **that's a load of old cobblers!**

cold as a witch's tit(**, as**) extremely cold. Used in the USA since the 1930s or earlier, and occasionally in the UK. The phrase also exists in the intensified form *colder than a witch's tit.*

cold enough to freeze the balls off a brass monkey refers to extremely cold weather. (In polite company, *ears* or *tail* may be substituted for *balls*.) The date of origin is unknown, and the derivation of the phrase has been the subject of some dispute. Naval historians claim that it dates back to the days when cannon-balls were stacked on a brass tray known as a monkey; intense cold would cause the metal to contract, and the pile of balls would collapse. However, the majority of users interpret the phrase more literally: the weather is so bitterly cold that it would freeze not only an ordinary monkey's testicles off, but even a metal one's. (This interpretation is sometimes associated with the popular statuette group of 'the three wise monkeys – hear no evil, see no evil, speak no evil', often made of brass, found in many early 20th-century households.) The phrase has given rise to a number of allusive or euphemistic variants, notably *brass-monkey weather*, and also the phrase *I wouldn't want to be a pawnbroker's sign on a night like this* (referring to the three metal balls of a pawnbroker's sign).

collapse of stout party applied to Victorian humour. Since around 1880. The origin of the phrase lies in the finale of a number of *Punch*'s verbosely captioned cartoons of the mid-19th century.

come again? what did you say?; what do you mean?; please repeat or explain that. The phrase is sometimes an expression of surprise or incredulity. Since around 1919.

come and get it! come and eat!; dinner (or lunch, tea, etc.) is served! The phrase probably originated in army camps of the 19th century. It is sometimes used in other contexts, as in the following extract from James Hadley Chase's novel *You're Dead without Money* (1972): '"Come and get it," she said and going to the bed, she lay down, swung up her long legs and beckoned to him.'

come back . . ., all is forgiven a jocularly despairing appeal to one who has left a particular post or organization in which his or her know-how would now be useful, or to somebody despised or disgraced who has been replaced by somebody worse, as in *come back, Margaret Thatcher, all is forgiven*. The phrase has been used in this way since around 1950. See also **come home, all is forgiven**.

come home, all is forgiven derives from a frequent advertisement in the 'agony column' of *The Times* in the late 19th and early 20th centuries. The phrase has given rise to the learned graffito 'Come home, Oedipus, all is forgiven. Love, Mother', which is usually followed by 'Over my dead body, Father'. See also **come back . . ., all is forgiven**.

come home with your knickers torn and say you found the money! (, **you**) do you expect me to believe that?; an expression of extreme scepticism. 20th century. Based on a (perhaps true) story of an irate mother addressing her errant teenage daughter.

come in, number six (or **four, eight,** etc.)**, your time is up**   applied to anybody who has had 'a good innings', a long career, etc. Since around 1950. The phrase was originally used by hirers of rowing-boats, etc.

come off your perch!   don't be so superior or high and mighty!; come down to earth! Variants include *come off the roof!* and *come off your horse!,* the latter deriving from the idiom *to come off one's high horse.*

come on in, the water's fine   a seaside cliché addressed as a catch phrase to any hesitant individual. Sometimes *lovely* replaces *fine.*

come to papa!   said by gamblers as they throw the dice; an entreaty for a winning throw. 20th century; chiefly used in the USA.

come up and see me sometime   a jocularly euphemistic sexual invitation. The phrase was probably already in general usage when it was popularized as the catch phrase of the US actress Mae West, who may or may not have said it in one of her plays or films: perhaps in the play *Diamond Lil* (1928). In the film *She Done Him Wrong* (1933) Mae West says to Cary Grant: 'Why don't you come up sometime and see me?'; in *My Little Chickadee* (1939) W. C. Fields says the phrase to Mae West in its now-famous, easier to articulate, form.

come up smelling of violets (or **roses**)   see **if he fell in the shit he'd come up smelling of violets** (or **roses**).

come up and see my etchings   a jocularly euphemistic sexual invitation. Probably of US origin, the phrase has been used in cartoons and jokes since the 1920s or earlier, perhaps from the late 19th century. The US humorist James Thurber turned the phrase on its head in the caption of a cartoon in *Men, Women and Dogs*: 'You wait here and I'll bring the etchings down.'

cool it!   calm down!; relax! Used in the US since around 1955 and in the UK from the late 1960s, the phrase is associated with Blacks, beatniks, and hippies. From the adjective *cool,* meaning 'unflustered', probably influenced by slang usage of the word.

cop (a load of) that lot!   just look at that (person or thing) or those (people or things)! An expression of astonishment or admiration (or, on the other hand, of contempt or derision). Used in Australia since around 1930; also used in the UK.

could eat the hind leg off a donkey(, I or **he,** etc.)   I'm (or he's, etc.) extremely hungry. Late 19th–20th centuries. Possibly a blend of the phrases *I could eat a horse* and *he could talk the hind leg off a donkey.*

couldn't give a monkey's   see **give a monkey's, couldn't** (or **doesn't**).

couldn't knock the skin off a rice-pudding(, you or **he,** etc.)   addressed or applied to a weakling or coward; an expression of extreme contempt. 20th century. Variants include *he couldn't fight his way out* *of a paper bag, you couldn't blow the froth off a pint,* etc.

couldn't organize a piss-up in a brewery(**, you** or **he**, etc.) applied with derision or contempt to somebody who is grossly inefficient or incompetent. Possibly from the 1920s or 1930s. A variant is *you* (or *he,* etc.) *couldn't organize a fuck in a brothel.*

count the spoons! said after the departure of a visitor (or visitors), with the (usually jocular) implication that this person is not to be trusted. Since the 1940s or earlier. On the UK radio programme *Stop the Week,* 17 October 1977, Anne Lesley remarked: 'It always makes me laugh because it implies . . . that you have spoons worth stealing.'

crazy mixed-up kid applied to a young person who is confusingly troubled with psychological problems, or with the problems of adolescence, as in *he's just a crazy mixed-up kid.* Of US origin, adopted in the UK in the late 1940s.

cross my palm with silver! (**, first**) a jocular request for a tip, bribe or other small payment where none is needed. Since the 1930s or earlier. From the gypsy fortune-teller's age-old request to a prospective client.

cry all the way to the bank used ironically by or of somebody whose work is adversely criticized on artistic, literary or musical grounds but who has had the temerity to make a fortune from it. Adopted from the USA in the late 1960s. The phrase is attributed to the colourful US pianist Liberace, who wrote in his *Autobiography* (1973): 'When the reviews are bad I tell my staff that they can join me as I cry all the way to the bank.' The more straightforward variant *laugh all the way to the bank* lacks the ironic subtlety of the original.

curtains for you (or **him**, etc.)!(**, it's**) it's the end for you/him/etc.! (referring to death, disablement, dismissal, imprisonment, etc.). In the form *curtains for you!,* or simply *curtains!,* the phrase also means 'that's enough (argument, talk, etc.) from you!' Used in the USA since around 1920; adopted in the UK around 1944. From the curtain that is dropped on the stage at the end of a play.

cut off my legs and call me Shorty! (**, well**) an exclamation of surprise, verging on disbelief. The phrase originated in the USA before 1945.

D

daddy, buy me one of those! a variant of the 19th-century catch phrase *I (really) must have one of those!* Since the early 20th century. Another variant, less frequent in the UK, has *mummy* in place of *daddy*.

damn white of you!, that's see **that's mighty** (or **damn**) **white of you!**

damned clever these Chinese! a jocular or ironic response to an explanation of some device or process; a somewhat back-handed compliment to Chinese inventiveness and ingenuity. The phrase may have originated in the USA in the 1930s or earlier; it was adopted in the UK during World War II. The variant *fiendish clever these Chinese* became a catch phrase of the radio series *The Goon Show* (first broadcast in 1952 in the UK). Other variants include *clever chaps* (or *devils*) *these Chinese!* and *darn clever these Armenians!*

dead, and never called me 'mother' said with ironic melodrama in any appropriate situation. The phrase is derived from the dramatized version (1874) of Mrs Henry Wood's novel *East Lynne.*

death-adders in your pocket?, have you got see **have you got a snake in your pocket?**

decisions, decisions! a jocular cry of anguish from one who has to make a decision, usually in the most trivial of circumstances, as in *'Would you like tea or coffee?' 'Oh, decisions, decisions!'* Since around 1955.

dedigitate! see **pull your finger out!**

depends on what you mean by see **it all depends. . ..**

did he fall or was he pushed? was his departure voluntary: did he resign or was he dismissed? The feminine form, with *she* in place of *he*, may also refer to loss of virginity, and both forms of the phrase are sometimes used in more literal contexts, expressing suspicion about an apparent accident. The phrase may have originated in a murder case of the early 20th century – that of Violet Charlesworth, found dead at the foot of a cliff near Beachy Head.

did it fall (or drop) off a lorry? see **it fell off the back of a lorry.**

did she fall or was she pushed? see **did he fall or was he pushed?**

did you say something? addressed to somebody who has just broken wind. Late 19th–20th centuries.

did you shoot it yourself? said jocularly or disapprovingly to a woman wearing an expensive-looking fur coat, jacket, etc. The phrase has gained currency with the growth of the anti-fur lobby.

didn't come down in the last shower, I (or **he**, etc.) I am (or he is, etc.) more experienced and shrewd than you think; said by or of somebody who is not easily fooled. Mainly used in Australia in the late 19th–20th centuries.

different ball game, it's a see **ball game, it's a different** (or **whole new**).

different strokes for different folks each to his own taste. Originally used by US Blacks, the phrase had entered general usage by around 1970. In the UK the word *folks* is sometimes replaced by *blokes*.

difficult we do at once; the impossible will take a little longer, the a catch phrase that was widely used in the armed forces in the 1940s; now often found on joke signs in civilian workplaces. It may have been adumbrated in Anthony Trollope's *Phineas Redux* (1874). A variant (since around 1945) is *the impossible we do at once; miracles take a little longer.*

dirty mind is a constant joy (or **a joy for ever**), **a** a pun on the famous line from Keats's *Endymion* (1818): 'A thing of beauty is a joy for ever.' The phrase has been used since Edwardian times.

ditto the same goes for me; I think so too; so do I. Used in the USA since around 1925 and subsequently adopted in the UK.

do I have to spell it out for you (or **draw you a diagram**)? surely it's clear (or obvious) enough?; said in exasperation to somebody who is being particularly obtuse (or, perhaps, naïve), as in *he's a con-man, a swindler – do I have to spell it out for you?* Since around 1950.

do me a favour! surely you don't expect me to believe that!; what an absurd suggestion! An example is *financial adviser? Do me a favour – he's just an insurance salesman!* The phrase is also used to add emphasis to such commands as 'go away!', 'stop talking!', etc., as in *do me favour – shut up!* Since the late 1940s. The ungrammatical variant *do us a favour!* is in occasional use.

do one for me see **have one for me**.

do tell! really!; indeed!; Said ironically or with affected incredulity. Used in the USA since 1820 or earlier.

do you come here often? the conventional advance made by a tongue-tied boy or young man in a dance-hall, etc., used jocularly as a catch phrase. Since around 1950. The phrase was popularized by the UK radio series *The Goon Show* (first broadcast in 1952), where it was usually met with the response *only in the mating season.*

do you know any other funny stories? see **have you any more funny stories?**

do you know something? see **d'you know something?**

do you know what? used to introduce a piece of information. The phrase is neatly explained and illustrated in Damon Runyon's *My Wife Ethel* (1939): 'The other night my wife Ethel was reading the paper and she says Joe do you know what? I says here Ethel why do you always start to say something by asking me a question? . . . Ethel says why Joe that is not a question at all. That is just to get you to notice me so I can tell you something.' The word *do* is often omitted, especially in British usage. In Australia (and, perhaps, elsewhere) a standard response to this non-question is *you're mad and I'm not.* See also **d'you know something?**

do you mind! an expression of reproach, indignation or expostulation; often spoken with emphasis on the word *do*, or with the intonation of a question. Since the early 1950s.

do you see what I see? used to express astonishment at the unexpected appearance of somebody or something. The phrase dates from 1942 or earlier.

do you think I'm made of money? said to an importunate borrower or to an extravagant spouse, child, etc. Late 19th–20th centuries. A variant of this rhetorical question is the exclamation *you must think I'm made of money!* See also **grow on trees.**

do you want jam on it? (or **on both sides**)? see **d'you want jam on both sides?; what do you want – jam on it?**

do your own thing! follow your own inclinations! A catch phrase of US hippies from the late 1950s; adopted in the UK around 1969. By 1980, the phrase had a dated ring to it.

Doctor Livingstone, I presume said on meeting a stranger (or even a friend), especially fortuitously or unexpectedly. (Another name is sometimes substituted for that of Doctor Livingstone.) The phrase was allegedly spoken in 1871 by Henry Morton Stanley, on meeting the missionary and explorer David Livingstone in Central Africa, having been sent there with a search party for the missing doctor. It would be interesting to know whether Stanley had seen or read Sheridan's play *The School for Scandal* (1777), which contains the line 'Mr Stanley, I presume', not long before he set out for Africa.

does a bear shit in the woods? obviously; of course. Said in response to a question to which the answer is an obvious 'Yes'. Also used in the form *do bears shit in the woods?* Of US origin; used in the UK since the 1970s or earlier. See also **is the Pope Catholic?**

does your mother know you're out? addressed in a sarcastic or derisive way to somebody displaying exceptional simplicity, or as a put-down to a swaggering or precocious young person. The phrase dates from 1838 or earlier: classical scholars have found a similar phrase in Ancient Greek.

doesn't everyone? see **aren't we all?**

doesn't give a monkey's see **give a monkey's, couldn't** (or **doesn't**).

doesn't it make you want to spit? said in disgust. The phrase was popularized in the late 1930s by the British comedian Arthur Askey, who used it in the UK radio series *Band Waggon* (despite the disapproval of Lord Reith, director-general of the BBC).

done up like a dog's dinner see **all dressed up like a Christmas tree.**

don't all speak at once! used by somebody whose offer, suggestion, request, etc., has been greeted with silence or a conspicuous lack of enthusiasm, as in *any volunteers? . . . don't all speak at once!* Since around 1880 or earlier.

don't ask! said by somebody in an awkward predicament, to fend off questions as to how he or she got into that situation: it would take too long to explain, and could be embarrassing as well. Used in the USA since around 1965 and subsequently in the UK.

don't ask *me*, I only live (or **work**) **here** a response by a subordinate to an outsider's inquiry, often indicating the subordinate's resentment at his or her subordination or the state of ignorance in which those in this position are kept. Used in the USA from around 1925; adopted in the UK by 1945. The phrase *don't ask me* may be replaced by *I don't know* or *I wouldn't know*. See also **I only work here**.

don't be filthy! don't be foul-mouthed (or bawdy or suggestive)! The phrase was popularized in the late 1930s by the British comedian Arthur Askey, in the UK radio series *Band Waggon*, but is not much heard in modern usage (since around 1960).

don't bet on it! see **I wouldn't bet on it!**

don't call us, we'll call you a polite brush-off or a gentle intimation of probable rejection, addressed, for example, to an interviewee. Since around 1945. The phrase originated in the world of the theatre or cinema (probably in the USA), where it was traditionally used at the end of an audition. The implication is, of course, that 'we' will never call 'you'.

don't come the (old) acid with me! don't be insolent (or unpleasant or sarcastic)!; stop throwing your weight about! Since the early 20th century.

don't come the (old) tin soldier with me! don't be so presumptuously impertinent! From the slang phrase *to come the old soldier*, which dates from the 19th century in the sense of 'to impose on'. A correspondent has noted the Glaswegian variant *don't come the little tin soldier with me, laddie, or I'll melt ye!*

don't come the raw prawn! addressed to somebody who is trying to put one over or impose on the speaker, or to somebody who is pretending to be naïve or innocent. Of Australian origin, the phrase arose during World War II.

don't do anything I wouldn't do! jocular valedictory advice, usually with sexual connotations. The traditional response is 'That gives me plenty of scope!' The phrase dates from around 1910 or earlier. See also **be good! – and if you can't be good, be careful!**

don't fire until you see the whites of their eyes a quotation from the War of American Independence, which became a catch phrase in the early 20th century. The original quotation, 'Men, you are all marksmen – don't one of you fire until you see the whites of their eyes', was an order issued by Israel Putnam (or William Prescott or Joseph Warren, such being the stuff of which history is made and the evidence from which so much of it has been written) to his troops at the Battle of Bunker Hill, 1775. As a catch phrase it is used in any metaphorically comparable situation.

don't fret! see **don't (you) fret!**

don't get mad, get even! revenge is more satisfying and effective than mere anger. Used in the USA since around 1965; also used in the UK.

don't get your knickers in a twist! don't get angry (or flustered or excited)! Addressed to a man, the phrase may imply that he is behaving like a flustered woman. 20th century. Variants of the phrase include *don't get your arse in an uproar!*

don't give me that! I don't believe that!; addressed to somebody who seems to take the speaker for a fool, as in *'I tried to phone you, but I got no reply.' 'Don't give me that – I was in all day and the phone never rang!'* Since around 1920.

don't go out of your way! an ironic admonition to somebody who is clearly reluctant to comply with an entirely reasonable request. The phrase has been used in the UK and the USA since around 1930 or earlier. *See also* **don't strain yourself**.

don't hold your breath! don't count on it!; Elliptical for 'don't hold your breath in expectation or excitement', referring to something that is unlikely to happen in the near future, if ever. The phrase may have originated during World War II.

don't I know it! how well I know it!; a somewhat rueful expression of the speaker's own (bitter) experience. The phrase has been used in the UK and the USA since around 1880 or earlier.

don't just stand there: do something! a literal exhortation to action that became a catch phrase around 1940. The phrase is sometimes jocularly reversed to *don't just do something: stand there!* or *don't do anything: just stand there!* The US comedian Bob Hope is alleged to have said to the striptease dancer Gipsy Rose Lee: 'Don't just stand there – undo something!'

don't keep a good woman waiting! jocular advice given in a social context, usually with sexual connotations. Late 19th–20th centuries.

don't knock it! don't criticize it: it may not be ideal, but it's by no means worthless, as in *'That's a rather old-fashioned method.' 'Don't knock it – it works!'* The phrase has been used in the USA since the late 1930s and is also used in the UK. The extended form *don't knock it if you haven't tried it* appeared in the 1960s.

don't let's play games! don't waste time fooling about; addressed to somebody who tries to evade the issue by quibbling or prevaricating. Probably since around 1945. The phrase *let's not play games!* is a frequent variant.

don't look now, but . . . used to draw attention to somebody or something, e.g. somebody who has just entered a restaurant: the speaker knows full well that the hearers are likely to turn round at once to look. The phrase is derived from the full form *don't look now, but I think we're being followed,* a jocular allusion to a timorous person's mostly imaginary fear, which dates from around 1933.

don't make a meal of it! said to somebody who is making a long story of or a great fuss about something trivial. From around 1950. The phrase is also used in the sense of **don't make a production of it!**

don't make a production of it! addressed to one who makes a simple matter seem difficult and/or very important. Since the late 1930s. From the theatrical or cinematic sense of the word *production.*

don't make waves! see **don't rock the boat!**

don't mind me! addressed ironically to somebody who is making a nuisance of himself or herself. Adopted from the USA around 1924, it was originally used in such phrases as *amuse yourself: don't mind me!,* said with an air of martyrdom to express one's hurt at being left out of some activity.

don't mock the afflicted! used in a variety of contexts, e.g. when somebody makes a blunder or bungles a job.

don't rock the boat! don't disturb the status quo!; used, for example, in political or economic contexts when somebody expresses a desire or intention to do something that would disturb the existing comfortable situation. Since around 1920. Variants include *don't make waves!* and *sit down, you're rocking the boat!,* the latter being the title and refrain of a song in the musical *Guys and Dolls.*

don't shit on your own doorstep(**, you**)   a warning against carrying on sexual intrigues at one's own place of work, residence, etc. Late 19th–20th centuries. The US equivalent is *never shit where you eat.* The phrase may also be a down-to-earth variant of the proverbial *(you) don't foul your own nest,* which refers to the vilification or disgrace of one's own family, country, etc.

don't shoot the pianist (– he's doing his best)!   a catch phrase derived from a notice originally displayed in saloons of the Wild West. Adopted from the USA around 1918. There are a number of variants, such as *don't shoot the piano-player . . .* and *please do not shoot the pianist . . ..* In his *Impressions of America,* Oscar Wilde commented on such a notice seen in a US bar-room during his tour of the USA.

don't some mothers have (or **'ave**) **'em!**   see **some mothers do 'ave** (or **have**) **'em!**

don't spend it all at once (or **in one shop**)   a jocular accompaniment to the handing over of a very small amount of money (or a single coin), especially as change. The phrase dates back to the late 19th century.

don't strain yourself!   an ironic admonition to somebody who is reluctant to co-operate with a reasonable request. The phrase was first used in Australia around 1913 and has been in use in the US and the UK since around the same period. *See also* **don't go out of your way!**

don't take any wooden nickels!   take care of yourself! This US catch phrase probably dates from around 1900 and was particularly popular during the 1920s. Also used in the UK.

don't tell me: let me guess!   an anticipatory catch phrase, often used with the implication 'you don't need to tell me, I already know (or can easily guess)'. Since around 1940.

don't we all?   see **aren't we all?**

don't worry: it may never happen   jocular advice to somebody who looks worried, unhappy or merely thoughtful, or to anybody whose natural expression is not a smile. Since around 1916. A variant is *cheer up: it may never happen.*

don't you forget it!   see **and don't you forget it!**

don't (you) fret!   you have no cause to worry: addressed sarcastically to somebody who is worrying needlessly. Late 19th–20th centuries.

don't you know there's a war on?   an admonition to those who waste time or resources, behave in a frivolous manner, make unreasonable requests, etc., as in *hurry up – don't you know there's a war on?* Used during World Wars I and II and jocularly thereafter. A less frequent variant is *remember there's a war on!*

doom and gloom(, gloom and doom) an expression of extreme pessimism. The phrase may have originated in the anti-nuclear anxiety of the 1950s–60s; it was popularized by the film *Finian's Rainbow* (1968), in which it is frequently repeated by the leprechaun (played by Tommy Steele). The second part of the phrase is sometimes used as a noun or adjectivally, as in *the report is not all gloom and doom.*

down, Fido (or **Rover**)! a woman's jocular command to a man to desist from intimate approaches. A US catch phrase of the 20th century, also used in the UK.

dressed up like a dog's dinner see **all dressed up like a Christmas tree.**

drop dead! an exclamation of refusal, rejection, dismissal, etc. Used in the USA from the late 1930s and in the UK since around 1949, often by teenagers. The full form *why don't you drop dead!* is a less frequent variant; *drop dead twice!* is an intensified form of the phrase.

duty calls! means 'excuse me, I must go to the lavatory.' Chiefly used by men (rather than women), the phrase originated in the armed forces around 1916 or earlier and entered civilian usage around 1919.

d'you know something? used to introduce a piece of information, or as a fairly meaningless tag, as in *d'you know something? I don't give a damn!* Adopted from the USA around 1945. See also **do you know what?**

d'you want jam on both sides? addressed to somebody making an unreasonable request. Since around 1916. The phrase is an elaboration of *do you want jam on it?* (see **what do you want – jam on it?**). The US equivalent is *d'you want egg in your beer?*

E

earwig! earwig! be quiet – there's somebody listening! From around 1830 to 1914 or later. A pun on the word *ear*, which has survived in the slang term *earwig*, meaning 'to eavesdrop' or 'eavesdropper'.

eat your heart out! doesn't that make you jealous or envious?; usually preceded (or followed) by the name of a famous person and used with jocular or ironic reference to a potential rival, as in *Madonna, eat your heart out!* Since the mid-1960s; adopted from the USA.

'eave 'arf a brick at 'im! a reflection of the prejudiced British lower-class attitude to foreigners. The phrase was in use from the mid-1850s to 1914, and is still occasionally heard in the later 20th century. It was inspired by a cartoon in *Punch*, 25 February 1854, an exchange between two miners regarding a gentleman walking past: '"Who's 'im, Bill?" "A stranger!" "'Eave 'arf a brick at 'im!"'

education has been sadly neglected, your see **your education has been sadly neglected**.

egg on (one's) face applied to somebody who has committed a social, political or commercial blunder and suffers humiliation or embarrassment, as in *to have* (or *get*) *egg on (one's) face*, *the prime minister is going to end up with egg on his face over this*. Adopted from the USA around 1973.

elementary, my dear Watson! it's really quite simple or obvious; often said with an air of smug superiority. A catch phrase of the Sherlock Holmes stories by Arthur Conan Doyle, used in the UK throughout the 20th century and also used in the USA. The phrase does not appear in this form in any of the stories themselves, though 'The Crooked Man' in *The Memoirs of Sherlock Holmes* (1894) contains the following exchange between Watson and Holmes (respectively): '"Excellent!" I cried. "Elementary," said he.' It has, however, been used in adaptations of Doyle's work, notably at the end of the first sound film version, *The Return of Sherlock Holmes* (1929).

English as she is spoke the poor English spoken by the illiterate, the semi-literate and the abominably careless. 20th century. The phrase originally referred to the broken English spoken by foreigners, and was probably derived from *English as she is spoke: or a Jest in sober earnest,* the title of a book (published in 1883) containing selections from a Portuguese-English conversational guide, including such gems as 'The walls have hearsay'.

enjoy your trip? said to somebody who stumbles. The phrase dates from around 1920. The variant *have a good trip?* is said to have been addressed by George VI to a BBC technician who fell over a cable during a photographic session at Buckingham Palace. A pun on the word *trip*, meaning 'stumble' or 'short journey or excursion'.

enough said! say no more! An expression of understanding or agreement. The phrase has been used since the mid-19th century in the phonetic shortened form *nuff said!*

enough to make a cat laugh very funny or ludicrous, as in *you should have seen him trying to dance – it was enough to make a cat laugh!* Since around 1820. The phrase has the variant *it would make a cat laugh*.

enough to piss off the Pope an expression of extreme anger, disgust, outrage, etc., as in *they keep fobbing me off with excuses – it's enough to piss off the Pope!* Since the 1960s. From the slang phrase *pissed off*, meaning 'angry, disgusted, etc.'.

even blind Freddie could see that see **blind Freddie could see that**.

even paranoids have real enemies see **just because you're paranoid, it doesn't mean to say they aren't all out to get you**.

every day and in every way from the slogan coined by Dr Emile Coué, originator of a psychotherapeutic system of autosuggestion in which patients were instructed to repeat as frequently as possible the formula: 'Every day, in every way, I am getting better and better.' The catch phrase was in vogue at the height of Coué's fame, in the early 1920s, and is still heard from time to time.

every home should have one applicable to almost any item, from common objects (as in *it's a great little machine: every home should have one*) to people, animals – and even non-material things. The phrase originated as an advertising slogan, probably in the 1920s.

every little helps, as the old woman said when she pissed in the sea said when one urinates into the sea (or a river or stream), or when making any tiny contribution to a cause, especially a collection of funds. Since the mid-19th century. The phrase is proverbial in origin, dating back to the 16th century in the form *everything helps, quoth the wren when she pissed into the sea*.

every silver lining has its cloud a pessimistic reversal of the famous proverb, coined by Noël Coward in a song of the late 1930s.

every time he opens his mouth he puts his foot in it said of one given to committing verbal blunders or making tactless remarks. Since around 1920 or earlier. The following remark on the subject is attributed to Prince Philip, Duke of Edinburgh: 'Dentopedology is the science of opening your mouth and putting your foot in it. I've been practising it for years.'

everybody say 'aah!'   a response to a tale of woe, lessening its impact. The commiserative sound *aah!* is uttered on a long falling tone. From the 1970s. The phrase seems to be the verbal equivalent of the gesture of playing a violin to indicate mock sorrow at a hard-luck story.

everything but the kitchen sink   virtually everything, as in *she seems to have brought everything but the kitchen sink with her.* The variant *everything including the kitchen sink* is sometimes used for emphasis. The phrase has been used in the UK and the USA throughout the 20th century, especially since around 1945. It has given rise to a number of sarcastic allusive remarks addressed e.g. to a person carrying a lot of luggage, filling the boot of a car, etc., such as 'Where's the kitchen sink?' or 'You've forgotten the kitchen sink!' (A variant of the latter is the catch phrase *you've forgotten the piano!*)

everything in the garden is lovely   all is going well. The phrase has been used since the early 20th century, possibly derived from (or popularized by) the title of a song.

everything's coming up roses   things are going very well. Since around 1950. The phrase was used as the title of a song by the US songwriter Stephen Sondheim in 1959.

everything's under control   applied to any situation where things are 'ticking over nicely'; also used to give reassurance when things appear to be going wrong, as in *don't worry: everything's under control.* The phrase dates from around 1930.

excuse my French!   see **pardon my French!**

excuse my pig: he's a friend!   said when a companion disgraces one, e.g. by belching or breaking wind; a jocular inversion of the words *friend* and *pig*. Since around 1950. See also **is he with you? . . .; you can't take him** (or **her**) **anywhere!**

expect me when you see me   see **I'll expect you when I see you.**

extract the manual digit!   see **pull your finger out!**

eyes like piss-holes in the snow   a graphic description of the appearance of somebody 'the morning after the night before', i.e. suffering from a hangover. Since around 1920.

F

face that would stop a clock, a applied unkindly and derisively to an ugly or formidable-looking person, especially a woman. The phrase has been in use since around 1890. A similar expression is *a face like the back of a bus* (or, earlier, *a tram*).

fair do's (or **doo's**) an appeal for equality of treatment, as in *fair do's: let everybody have a go*. The phrase is probably a corruption of *fair dues*, which dates back to 1880 or earlier. It is sometimes extended to *fair do's all round*.

fair enough! that sounds reasonable; I'll accept that; an expression of general agreement. The phrase is also used as a question, meaning 'is that agreeable to you?' From the 1920s. In the mid-1940s the phrase gave rise to the appalling pun: 'I am a fairy. My name is Nuff. I'm the . . .'.

fair go! be fair!; be reasonable!; a protest against unfair treatment or a plea for fair treatment. Mainly used in Australia; possibly since around 1908 or earlier. The phrase comes from the gambling game of two-up.

fair to middling a jocular reply to such questions as 'How are you?' or 'How's it going?' The phrase means 'about average', *fair* and *middling* being virtually synonymous. It has been in colloquial usage since the early 20th century. Similarly non-committal responses include *can't complain* and *mustn't grumble*.

fame at last! used ironically in a variety of occupational or social contexts, e.g. when one's name is seen or heard in connection with something of minor importance or something unpleasant. The catch phrase dates from around 1946.

family, hold back (or **off**)**!** a domestic catch phrase of the middle classes, warning members of the family (when guests are present) that there is not enough of a particular dish for all. For obvious reasons, the phrase is usually abbreviated to *f.h.b.* (or *f.h.o.*, also interpreted as *family, hands off!*). Since the mid-19th century. Corollaries of the phrase include *m.i.k.* (= more in kitchen) and *f.t.i.* (= family, tuck in!).

famous last words! a rejoinder to such fatuous statements as 'It's perfectly safe!' or 'Nothing can possibly go wrong!'; a jocular or derisive reference to the 'famous last words' of history, such as 'It could never happen in this country!' The phrase has been in general usage since around 1945. It is sometimes used allusively, as in Karen Campbell's *Suddenly in the Air* (1969): 'I smiled. "We're doing remarkably well." These were famous last words.'

fate worse than death, a a cliché applied jocularly or ironically to any unpleasant or undesirable situation, as in *he was faced with the prospect of having to work for his living – a fate worse than death*. Since the mid-18th century it has been used with specific reference to the rape or seduction of a girl or young woman.

feeding time at the zoo applied to any disorderly scene, not necessarily involving food and drink, as in *on the first day of the sales it's like feeding time at the zoo*. Possibly since the late 1940s.

feel free! a benevolently generous reply to somebody who has asked to do something, as in *'May I close the window?' 'Feel free!'* Used in the USA from the early 1950s and in the UK since the 1960s. The phrase is virtually synonymous with **be my guest!**

feeling no pain drunk, with the intention of becoming incapable; a response to the question 'How are you?' Since around 1945. Perhaps from the verse: 'I feel no pain, dear mother, now / But oh, I am so dry! / Please lead me to a brewery / And leave me there to die', a parody of the opening lines of Edward Farmer's poem *The Collier's Dying Child*: 'I have no pain, dear mother, now; / But oh! I am so dry; / Just moisten poor Jim's lips once more; / And mother, do not cry!'

fifty million Frenchmen can't be wrong a reference to sexual intercourse, extolling its virtues. From a popular song of World War I. The phrase has been adapted for used in other contexts, with reference to other things.

fine weather for ducks! extremely wet weather; a jocular comment made on a very rainy day. The phrase has been used in this form since the late 19th century. Variants of the phrase include *nice* (or *lovely, great*, etc.) *weather for ducks!*, *fine weather if you're a duck!* and *a fine day for the ducks!*

finger of suspicion points at you!, the a cliché of old-style crime stories, used jocularly as a catch phrase, often in the most trivial circumstances. Since around 1925.

fings ain't wot they used t'be an expression of nostalgia, usually said by (or, mockingly, to) one who sees the past through rose-coloured spectacles. The phrase was popularized in this form as the title of a musical (1959) by Frank Norman and Lionel Bart, having originated as the title of song by Ted Persons and Mercer Ellington, 'Things Ain't What They Used To Be' (1941). The general sentiment behind the phrase probably goes back centuries.

first catch your hare don't act prematurely; a counterpart of the proverb 'don't count your chickens before they are hatched'. The phrase is thought to have originated as a the first line of a recipe, and is often regarded as a misquotation of the culinary instruction given by Hannah Glasse in her book *The Art of Cookery Made Plain and Easy* (1747): 'Take your hare when it is cased [i.e. skinned] . . .'. However, the *Oxford Dictionary of Proverbs* suggests that the phrase was in general use as early as the 14th century.

fish, or cut bait! finish what you're doing (or trying to do), or stop and give somebody else the chance to (try to) do it! The phrase originated in the USA around 1876. It is virtually synonymous with the more frequent **shit** (or **piss**), **or get off the pot!**

flattery will get you nowhere you won't succeed in persuading me by flattering me, as in *'Will you have a look at my car – you're so good at fixing things!' 'Flattery will get you nowhere!'* Since around 1945 or earlier. The phrase is sometimes used ironically, in response to an uncomplimentary remark. It also has the jocular variant *flattery will get you everywhere*, often said with sexual innuendo.

fleet's lit up!, the the origin of this catch phrase is attributed to Lieutenant Commander Thomas Woodrooffe, in his BBC radio commentary on the fleet illuminations at the Spithead Coronation Naval Review on 20 May 1937. According to the BBC staff magazine *Ariel* (7 July 1977): 'When the time came for him to go on the air, he could produce just one comment, "The fleet is all lit up," which he repeated five times.' However, Woodrooffe's actual commentary is believed to have begun: 'At the present moment, the whole fleet's lit up. When I say "lit up", I mean lit up by fairy lamps.' The cause of this famous broadcasting bloomer has also been the subject of some dispute: Woodrooffe is said to have delivered the commentary after celebrating with some old shipmates, but he later denied drunkenness, blaming a combination of nervous exhaustion and emotion for his confusion. The phrase was subsequently used as the title of a show and a popular song.

flings money around like a man with no arms see **he flings** (or **throws**) **money around like a man with no arms.**

floats like a brick-built shithouse applied to a ship that is very slow because it is so heavily built; used in the Merchant Navy since around 1950. Probably from the phrase **built like a brick shithouse.**

fools seldom differ see **great minds think alike.**

for my next trick   (followed by a significant pause) said by somebody who has just made a mess of things, or by an onlooker. Probably since around 1900. The phrase originated in the world of entertainment, uttered by a magician or conjuror, and was subsequently used as a comic apology after any minor mishap on stage.

for obvious reasons   used in a situation where the reasons are not at all obvious, for bafflement or mere padding, or as a parody of its literal, rather patronizing, usage. Since the mid-1970s.

for the hell of it   for no particular reason; simply for the pleasure of doing it, experiencing it, etc. The phrase may have originated in the USA around 1910, and was probably adopted in the UK in the early 1940s. Elaborations of the phrase include *just for the hell of it* and *for the sheer hell of it.*

for the man who has everything   applied to a conspicuously useless (and usually expensive) item intended as a gift; said in mockery of the item itself or of advertisements that use the phrase literally and seriously. The advertising slogan originated in the USA in the 1950s and soon became a catch phrase; it is also used in the UK.

for this relief, much thanks!   uttered after (or during) a much-needed urination. Used as a catch phrase since the late 19th century. The phrase originated in the opening scene of Shakespeare's *Hamlet*, said by a sentinel to his replacement: 'For this relief much thanks; 'tis bitter cold / And I am sick at heart.'

for those few kind words, thank you (or **many thanks**)   see **thank you for those few kind words**.

for what we are about to receive   a naval catch phrase, uttered by the crew of a ship awaiting a broadside; also used in general contexts in anticipation of anything unpleasant. Since the mid-18th century. From the grace said before meals: 'For what we are about to receive, may the Lord make us truly thankful.'

for your information   introduces a sarcastic, indignant, or supercilious response to an impertinent question or remark, as in *'What do you know about such things?' 'For your information, I'm a qualified accountant!'* Used as a catch phrase since around 1955, with ironic allusion to the legitimate queries of commerce and bureaucracy.

forget it!   it's not worth worrying about (as in *'How much do I owe you?' 'Forget it!'*); don't even think about it (as in *if you're planning to go by car, forget it – there's nowhere to park*); also said in exasperation to one who seems unable to grasp what the speaker is trying to explain. Used in the USA since the 1930s and in the UK since around 1950.

from the sublime to the gorblimey   from the sublime to the ridiculous; used as an occasional variant of this cliché since the 1920s or earlier. From the Cockney slang exclamation *gorblimey!*, a corruption of 'God blind me!'

fuck a duck!   see **go fuck a duck!**

fuck 'em all!   an expression of (usually cheerful) defiance, applied to the world in general or to a particular circumstance or situation. Since around 1919. An extended variant is *fuck 'em all bar six, and they can be the pall-bearers.*

fuck 'em and chuck 'em   epitomizes a certain basic male attitude to the opposite sex. The phrase dates back to the 19th century in the form *fuck 'em and leave 'em*, used by members of the armed forces. It may have originated as a coarsening and vulgarization of **I must love you and leave you**. The 'mechanized' variant *screw and bolt*, which dates from the late 1920s, gave rise to a joke headline for a newspaper story about a madman who raped several laundresses and then disappeared: 'Nut screws washers and bolts'.

fuck that (or **this**) **for a lark!**   an expression of extreme dissatisfaction or disgust at some uncongenial task, situation, suggestion, etc., as in *fuck this for a lark – I'm going home!* A catch phrase of the 20th century. A frequent variant is *fuck that* (or *this*) *for a game of soldiers*, which originated in the armed forces in the late 1940s and is now in general use.

fuck you, Jack, I'm all right   epitomizes the arrogant, complacent, selfish or uncaring attitude of those in a superior position towards those less fortunate than themselves, e.g. senior officers to other ranks, management to workers, rich to poor, employed to unemployed, etc. The phrase probably dates from around 1880 in nautical usage. (Its adoption by the army caused the Royal Navy to coin the variant *fuck you, Jack, I'm inboard*; not to be outdone, the RAF came up with *fuck you, Jack, I'm fire-proof.*) The bowdlerized variant *I'm all right, Jack* is probably more frequent in general usage, having been popularized as the title of a successful comedy film (1959) starring Peter Sellers and Ian Carmichael.

fucked by the fickle finger of fate   down on one's luck; blighted by an unexpected stroke of misfortune; done for. Used in the USA from around 1930 and in the UK since 1960 or earlier. The phrase *fickle finger of fate* is sometimes used alone, popularized by the US television series *Rowan and Martin's Laugh-In* (first broadcast in 1967, also in the UK), in which the Flying Fickle Finger of Fate was a prize awarded to the winner of a mock talent contest. The variant *diddled by the dangling dong of destiny* seems not to have caught on, in spite of its imitative alliteration.

full stop, end of story!   indicates the (perhaps sudden or unexpected) end of an incident, matter, statement, story, etc., as in *do that once more and you'll be out on your ear: full stop, end of story!*; *one night he came home late from the pub and she walked out and left him: full stop, end of story!* Since the late 1950s or early 1960s. The variant *full stop!* (which may be an abbreviation or the original form of the catch phrase) has a wider range of usage, as in *I'm a failed teacher, a failed writer: I'm just a failure, full stop!*

funny peculiar or funny ha-ha?   a query prompted by any potentially ambiguous use of the word *funny* (meaning 'amusing' or 'odd'), as in *'Something funny happened today.' 'Funny peculiar or funny ha-ha?'* The phrase has been in general use since around 1924. One of the earliest dependable examples of usage occurs in the third act of Ian Hay's play *Housemaster* (1938): 'What do you mean, funny? Funny peculiar or funny ha-ha?' The two elements of the phrase are sometimes transposed to form the variant *funny ha-ha or funny peculiar?*

funny thing happened (to me) on the way to the theatre, a   a traditional stage comedian's introduction to a joke, probably of music-hall or vaudeville origin. Other words may be substituted for *theatre*, as in the title of the musical *A Funny Thing Happened on the Way to the Forum* (1962; filmed in 1966) and, earlier, in a speech made by Adlai Stevenson after losing the US presidential election of 1952: 'A funny thing happened to me on the way to the White House.'

fur coat and no knickers   see **red hat and no knickers**.

G

gangway! clear a passage!; stand back!; get out of the way!; an order to make way for somebody or something (e.g. somebody important, somebody on an urgent mission, somebody pushing a trolley or carrying a tray of drinks, etc.). Of nautical origin, the phrase is now used in a wide range of general contexts.

garbage in, garbage out a catch phrase from the world of computing: if what is fed into the machine is rubbish, then rubbish is what will be churned out. Since the 1960s or earlier; sometimes used in non-computing contexts. The phrase is often abbreviated to *GIGO*, pronounced with a hard initial *g* and a long *i*.

geese flying out of one's backside, like see **like sparrows** (or **geese**) **flying out of one's backside.**

get lost! go away and stop bothering me! Adopted from the USA around 1949. The phrase is also used (along with *get knotted!*, *get stuffed!*, etc.) as an exclamation of rejection or refusal, as in '*Can you lend me a fiver?*' '*Get lost!*'

get off my case! leave me alone! Chiefly used by US Blacks in the late 1960s-70s.

get off my cloud! stop bothering me! The phrase was popularized among young people in the 1960s by the Rolling Stones' song 'Get Off Of My Cloud', which reached the top of the hit-parade in 1965.

get stuck in! an exhortation to work or play harder; used in sporting and general contexts. The phrase has been used in this sense in Australia and New Zealand since around 1920, and was subsequently adopted in the UK. It is also used (in the later 20th century) as an exhortation to tuck into one's food, as in *here's your dinner: get stuck in!*

get the lead out of your pants! get up and get busy!; also used as a synonym of **get stuck in!** The phrase originated in the USA around 1930. It is sometimes shortened to *get the lead out!* See also **shake the lead out of your ass!**

get *you*! addressed to a conceited person, with the aim of deflating his or her ego. Since the late 1950s. The phrase may also be used of a third person, with *him* or *her* in place of *you*.

get your act together! get yourself (or yourselves) organized! The

phrase has been used in the USA since the 1960s and was subsequently adopted in the UK. It is probably of show-business origin.

get your ass in gear! get moving!; start working! Used in the USA
since the 1960s or earlier. This is one of a number of colourful
expressions in which the phrase *your ass* is used in the sense of
'yourself'; others include *get your ass in* (or *out of*) *here!*

get your finger out! see **pull your finger out!**

getting any (lately)? a catch phrase used by men, especially on one
meeting another; the word *any*, of course, refers to sex. (Variants of
the phrase substitute *enough* or *much* for *any*.) Since the 1930s or
earlier. There are a number of standard responses, all used jocularly
or facetiously, such as 'climbing trees to get away from it', 'so busy
I've had to put a man on (to help me)' and 'have to fight them off
at the traffic lights'.

ghost walks on Friday, the a reference to pay-day. Of theatrical origin,
the phrase dates back to the 1840s. Probably an allusion to the ghost
in Shakespeare's *Hamlet*, perhaps from a time when this role was
played by the company business manager. Related phrases include
the ghost does not walk (meaning 'there is no money for wages'), *has
the ghost walked yet?*, and *when will the ghost walk?*

gissa (or **gizza**) **job!** give us (i.e. me) a job!; a catch phrase of the
character Yosser Hughes in Alan Bleasdale's *Boys from the Blackstuff*
(first broadcast in 1982), a series of television plays about unemploy-
ment in Liverpool. The phrase is often preceded or followed by *I
can* (or *could*) *do that!*

git there fustest with the mostest! a recipe for military success, occasionally applied in general contexts to anything that requires speed
and concentration of forces. Of US origin, the phrase is attributed
to General Nathan Bedford Forrest, explaining his success at Mur-
freesboro (1862) during the American Civil War, but historians aver
that Forrest would never have expressed himself in such sub-literate
terms. An alternative (and more likely) version of Forrest's actual
words is 'I just took the short cut and got there first with the most
men.'

give a monkey's, couldn't (or **doesn't**) applied to somebody who acts
without care or consideration for the consequences, or for other
people. A shortening of the phrase . . . *a monkey's fuck* (or *toss*); since
around 1970. The phrase is one of many similar expressions of the
form *(sb) couldn't* (or *doesn't*) *give* (or *care*) *a damn/two hoots/*etc.

give it a whirl! try it; it's worth trying, as in *go on, give it a whirl!; it may
not work, but let's give it a whirl!* Since the 1930s or earlier.

give me some skin! let's shake hands (especially with one person's flat palm brushing or slapping the other's flat palm). Used in the USA since around 1935, the phrase is often associated with Black or jazz usage.

give me strength! an exclamation of exasperation, especially at the folly, stupidity, incompetence or clumsiness of others. Since around 1920; perhaps of Australian origin. The phrase is short for *God give me strength (and patience)!*

give the cat another goldfish! let's be devils – damn the expense! Since the 1940s or earlier. The phrase occurs in John Wainwright's *Pool of Tears* (1977): "'What do you think, Lenny . . . a hundred?' – 'Two hundred,' said Lennox. 'Let's go wild – give the cat another goldfish.'" A variant of the phrase is *kill another canary and give the cat a treat!*

gizza job! see **gissa** (or **gizza**) **job!**

gloom and doom see **doom and gloom(, gloom and doom)**.

go (and) boil your head! don't be silly! A catch phrase of the 20th century.

go (and) chase yourself! go away and stop bothering me! Used in the USA since around 1910 or earlier; also used in the UK.

go (and) jump in the lake! an exclamation of dismissal, rejection or refusal. The phrase dates back to 1912 at the latest. See also **take a running jump at yourself!**

go and play in the traffic! go away and stop bothering me!; often addressed facetiously to a troublesome child. The phrase has been used in Scotland and elsewhere since the 1950s.

go and see a taxidermist! a variant of *get stuffed!* (see **get lost!**). The phrase may have originated in the armed forces around 1943, and is still used in civilian life.

go boil your head! see **go (and) boil your head!**

go chase yourself! see **go (and) chase yourself!**

go fly a kite! go away and do something else! The phrase was probably adopted from the USA in the mid-20th century.

go fuck a duck! go away!; get out of here!; a rhyming variant of *go fuck yourself!* Used in the USA since the 1920s; also used in the UK. The similar phrase *(cor* (or *gawd,* etc.),) *fuck a duck!* is an exclamation of surprise, dismay, irritation or annoyance.

go jump in the lake! see **go (and) jump in the lake!**

go to the top of the class! said to somebody who has answered quickly and correctly. Possibly of US origin; used in the UK since around 1948 or earlier.

God is alive and well and living in . . . see **alive and well and living in . . ..**

going in and out like a fiddler's elbow a description of anybody who seems jumpy or unsettled. An Anglo-Irish phrase of the 20th century.

going to hell in a hand-basket, the world's (or **he's, she's,** etc.) nothing is all right any more; we're sinking fast! Used in the USA since the 1920s.

gone for a Burton dead, absent, missing, lost, broken, useless, etc., as in *he's gone for a Burton; my calculator's gone for a burton.* (In modern usage *Burton* is often spelt with a lower-case *b.*) The phrase probably originated during World War II, when it was applied, for example, to a pilot who was missing or killed in action. (Partridge disputes but does not dismiss the theory that the phrase was used during World War I.) It is not known whether *Burton* refers to a glass of Burton ale or a suit made by Burton's the tailors (or neither): the former could be an allusion to 'the drink' (i.e. the sea, a pilot's or sailor's watery grave), the latter to 'a wooden suit' (i.e. a coffin).

good in parts, like the curate's egg applied to something that is not altogether bad. It is an allusion to a cartoon that appeared in *Punch* in 1895, featuring a curate taking breakfast in his bishop's home, with the following exchange between bishop and curate: "'I'm afraid you've got a bad egg, Mr Jones." "Oh no, my lord, I assure you! Parts of it are excellent!"' The phrase *like the curate's egg* sometimes stands alone.

good night! an exclamation of incredulity, despair, delight, surprise, anger, disgust, etc.; also used in the sense of 'that's done it!' or 'that's the end!' The phrase has been in general use in the UK from around 1880 (and in the USA from around 1910), but has declined in frequency since the mid-1930s.

good place to be from, (it's) a a veiled criticism of somebody's birth-place or home town, considered by the speaker to be a good place to get away from, as in *'I'm from Liverpool.' 'That's a good place to be from.'* Used in the USA since the 1950s; also used in the UK. Variants of the phrase include *(it's) a nice place to live out of.*

good question! see **that's a good question!**

good thinking! that's an excellent idea!; what a wonderful suggestion! Of US origin, used as a catch phrase in the UK since the 1960s. The phrase is sometimes extended to *good thinking, Batman!*, from the Batman comic strip (further popularized by the television series).

good time was had by all, a a catch phrase attributed to the British poet Stevie Smith, who used it as the title of a book of verse published in 1937. Partridge wrote to Stevie Smith shortly before her death in 1971 and asked her whether she had coined the phrase. Her reply was startlingly simple: she took it from parish magazines, where a church outing or social evening almost inevitably generated the comment 'A good time was had by all.'

got it in one!   said to somebody who has guessed the answer at the first attempt, or who has grasped the point straight away; often used ironically, when the answer or point is obvious. Used in the USA since around 1930 and subsequently adopted in the UK.

great minds think alike   said when two people have the same idea, share the same opinion, etc. (An unimpressed third party may add *(and) fools seldom differ.*) The catch phrase has been in general use since around 1880 or 1890, but the proverbial notion behind it may date back to the 17th century or earlier.

greatest thing since sliced bread   see **best thing since sliced bread, the.**

Greeks had a word for it, the   refers to any concept, thing, person, etc., that is unconventional but by no means novel. The phrase was coined by the US dramatist Zoë Akins, who used it in 1929 as the title (and in the original dialogue) of a play, with reference to a 'free spirit'. It caught on as a catch phrase with notable celerity in the USA and was almost instantaneously adopted in the UK.

grow on trees, it doesn't (or **they don't**)   an exasperated reply to a request made by one who seems to think that the thing in question (usually money) is always and immediately available or, at worst, very easily obtained, as in *no, you can't have more pocket money – it doesn't grow on trees, you know!* Late 19th–20th centuries. See also **do you think I'm made of money?**

grow up!   said to somebody who is behaving in a childish or ridiculous manner. The phrase has been used in the UK since the late 1930s; possibly of US origin. See also **act your age!; be your age!**

H

ha bloody ha! a sarcastic response to any stupid question or remark, or to a feeble joke or observation. Since around 1950. The phrase occurs in Dick Francis's thriller *Risk* (1977): 'If I hadn't gone suddenly blind (and it didn't feel like it), I was lying somewhere where no light penetrated. Brilliant deduction. Most constructive. Ha bloody ha.' The variant *ha fucking ha!* is used in less 'polite' circles.

half past kissing time and time to kiss again a reply given by a man to a woman who asks him the time. The phrase comes from a popular song of the 1880s: 'It's half-past kissing-time, and time to kiss again. / For time is always on the move, and ne'er will still remain; / No matter what the hour is, you may rely on this: / It's always half-past kissing-time, and always time to kiss.' The phrase is also sometimes addressed to children who continually ask 'What's the time?' Other jocular replies to this question include *half past three quarters(, and if you want to be hanged I'll lend you me garters)* and, especially in the USA, *half past my elbow (or ass) and a quarter to my thumb (or bum)*.

hand it to you, I have (or **I've got**) **to** said in recognition of the skill or superiority of the person addressed; sometimes ironic, as in *I have to hand it to you – nobody else could have made quite such a mess of things in such a short space of time!* 20th century; probably of US origin. The phrase is also used in other tenses and persons, as in *you had to hand it to him – he was a really smooth operator!*

hang in there! a cry of encouragement addressed, for example, to somebody doing a good job in difficult circumstances, or to anybody who seems downhearted. The phrase is associated with the hippies of the 1960s, but it may have originated earlier in the world of sport, addressed encouragingly to a player or team whom the odds are against.

hang loose! take it easy – relax!; shed all your inhibitions! Used in the USA since the mid-1950s and subsequently adopted in the UK.

happy as a bastard on Father's Day(**, as**) very unhappy. Used in Australia since around 1950. A variant of this simile substitutes *lucky* for *happy*.

happy as a pig in shit(, as) blissfully happy or contented. (There is no implication that the person so described has any other piggish characteristics.) 19th–20th centuries.

hard cheese! bad luck!; sometimes a sincere expression of commiseration, but more often used unsympathetically. Since the late 19th century. Perhaps from a gourmet's preference for soft cheese, or from the Persian and Hindi *chiz*, meaning 'thing'. See also **tough shit!; tough titty!**

hard act to follow see **act to follow, a hard** (or **tough**).

has the cat got your tongue? said to somebody (especially a child) who refuses to speak or to answer a question, or who is tongue-tied or speechless with embarrassment, shyness, surprise, fear, etc. Used in the UK and the USA since the mid-19th century. The phrase is often shortened to *cat got your tongue*, as in *what's the matter – cat got your tongue?*

has the ghost walked yet? see **ghost walks on Friday, the.**

has the penny dropped? do you now understand what was meant, or what needs to be done? Since the 1930s or earlier. See **penny has dropped, the.**

have a good trip? see **enjoy your trip?**

have a heart! don't be so hard-hearted! The phrase has been in general use since around 1880.

have at you! take this (or that)!; look out for yourself (or yourselves)!; uttered in defiance or challenge. The phrase was frequently used in the literature of the 16th–18th centuries, as in Shakespeare's *Love's Labour's Lost*: 'Have at you, then, affection's men-at-arms!' In more recent usage the catch phrase is usually playful or jocular. The word *you* may be replaced by *thee* or *ye* in historical or mock-historical contexts.

have gun, will travel I'm ready (or game) for anything. The phrase originally appeared in the personal column of *The Times*, where it was entirely serious; it was promoted to the status of a catch phrase in the early 20th century. The phrase was further popularized in the UK in the late 1950s and early 1960s, when it was used as the title of a US television series about a retired gunfighter who hires himself out. It has also given rise to an infinite number of frivolous adaptations, slogans, headings for book or film reviews, etc., such as *have bed, will travel, have wife, must travel, have pen, will write*, etc.

have I got news for you! I have something to tell you that you will find startling or unwelcome; a more emphatic version of **I've got news for you!** The phrase dates from the 1950s or earlier. In the early 1990s it was used as the title of a UK television news-quiz series.

have one for me addressed to somebody going to the pub, or to somebody going to the lavatory. (In the latter sense *do one for me* is a variant.) A catch phrase of the 20th century.

have you any more funny stories? tell me another! An expression of ironic scepticism or boredom. Since the late 1920s or early 1930s. Variants include *do you know any other funny stories?* and *now tell me the one about the three bears.*

have you got a snake in your pocket? addressed to one who is reluctant (and/or very slow) to buy a round of drinks when his turn has come. The implication is, of course, that the snake will bite his hand when he reaches into his pocket for his money. Mainly used in Australia; since around 1920. A variant of the phrase replaces *a snake* with *death-adders.*

have you heard any good stories lately? a social gambit. The phrase dates from around 1930, and was used in Noël Coward's play *Relative Values* (1951). It is sometimes shortened to *heard any good stories lately?* or *heard any good ones lately?* See also **read any good books lately?**

have you heard the latest? a jocular catch phrase to which the rejoinder, with or without a pause to enable one's interlocutor or audience to say 'No, tell me', is *it's not out yet!* 20th century.

have you *quite* finished? addressed sarcastically to one who is complaining or adversely criticizing or merely rambling pointlessly on and on. Since the 1920s or earlier. A variant is *when you've* quite *finished* ('we can get on' being understood).

having a wonderful time – wish you were here a cliché scrawled on a holiday postcard; often used facetiously or ironically (as among soldiers serving in the grim, wet, cold trenches of World War I). Since the 1870s or 1880s. The phrase *wish you were here* often stands alone, and has been used as the title of a musical comedy (1952) and a film (1987), both set in holiday resorts. It is sometimes altered for humorous effect, e.g. to *wish I weren't here*, and *wish you weren't here* (in the heading of a newspaper report about a controversial MP at the Liberal Party conference in Southport).

having fun? addressed ironically to somebody who is obviously having difficulties or in trouble. The phrase has been in use since around 1950.

he can make it sit up and beg refers to somebody who has become exceptionally skilful in working some material. The phrase may have originated among metal workers; it has been used in this sense since around 1920 or 1930. (In an earlier catch phrase it referred to an erection of the penis.) From the act of teaching a dog to sit up and beg for food.

he can put his shoes under my bed any time he likes I find him sexually attractive or acceptable. A catch phrase used by women, chiefly in Australia, since around 1920.

he can't tell shit from Shinola see **can't tell shit from Shinola.**

he flings (or throws) money around like a man with no arms applied to somebody who is exceptionally close-fisted. Used in the UK and Australia since around 1930. See also **have you got a snake in your pocket?**

he (or **she**) **has cloth ears** see **cloth ears, he** (or **she**) **has.**

he (or **she**) **has seen something nasty in the woodshed** see **something nasty in the woodshed, he** (or **she**) **has seen.**

he promised her the world, with a little red fence around it see **she wants the whole world, with a little red fence around it.**

he thinks it's just to pee through applied to an unsophisticated young man, implying inexperience (or even ignorance) of the alternative use of the organ in question. 20th century.

he thinks the sun shines out of (sb's) arsehole see **thinks the sun shines out of (sb's) arsehole, he** (or **she**).

he went thataway see **went thataway, he** (or **they**).

he who smelt it dealt it a juvenile riposte addressed to anybody who sniffs suspiciously when someone has broken wind, and says 'Who was that?' A less frequent variant is *he who denied it supplied it.* Both phrases have been in general use since around 1960.

he'd fuck a snake if he could get it to hold still he is spectacularly randy (implicitly from deprivation). The phrase may have originated in the Wild West, in the early 20th century. See also **he'd fuck anything on two legs.**

he'd fuck anything on two legs he has a reputedly spectacular sexual urge and potency; he is an inveterate womanizer; often said admiringly. Variants of the phrase substitute *shag* for *fuck* and replace *anything on two legs* with *anything that can walk, anything with a hole in it, anything from seventeen to seventy,* etc. Since the late 19th century. See also **he'd fuck a snake if he could get it to hold still.**

he'll take off any minute now he's extremely excited, agitated, or angry. An allusion to departing aircraft, the phrase originated in the RAF around 1938.

he's had a smell of the barman's apron applied to somebody who gets drunk very easily. Since around 1910. In the later 20th century, a more frequent variant is *one sniff at the barmaid's apron and he's away.*

heads I win, tails you lose a mock wager, in which the speaker cannot fail; often applied to an inequitable situation, as in *when it comes to borrowing money from these people, it's heads they win, tails you lose.* The phrase has been in general use since around 1830 or earlier, and was anticipated by Thomas Shadwell in *Epsom Wells* (1672): 'Worse than *Cross I win, Pile you lose*'.

heard any good ones (or **stories**) **lately?** see **have you heard any good stories lately?**

hello, hello, hello! the traditional policeman's comment upon an untoward incident or situation, used allusively as a catch phrase. Probably since around 1945 or 1946. In general usage the initial *h*'s are often dropped. There is a story of a young police officer who, on returning home unexpectedly early and finding his wife in bed with three men, exclaims, 'Hello, hello, hello!', causing her to burst into tears and sobbingly reproach him with the words, 'Darling, you didn't say hello to *me*!' See also **now then, what's all this 'ere?**

hello, sailor! often addressed to a homosexual male, alluding to the ambivalent sexuality of some sailors; also (perhaps originally) addressed by dockland prostitutes to potential customers. The phrase was used in the UK radio series *The Goon Show* in the 1950s, and was particularly popular during the mid-1970s.

help yourself! please do!; please yourself!; just as you please!, as in '*May I have a look?' 'Help yourself!'; 'I'd like to ask you a few questions.' 'Help yourself!'* Since around 1917.

hence the pyramids either applied to an unintentional non sequitur, or said ironically or jocularly as a deliberate non sequitur. Since the late 19th century. It derives from the very rude, very droll recitation known as *The Showman*.

here am I, slaving over a hot stove all day a jocular or ironic reproach addressed, for example, by a housewife to her husband (or children), as in *here am I, slaving over a hot stove all day, while all* you *do is sit at a desk*. It is now often used ironically by people who are not housewives when they are cooking an occasional meal. The phrase was used around 1910 in the title of a drawing by the caricaturist Art Young: 'Here am I, standin' over a hot stove all day, and you workin' in a nice, cool sewer!'

here endeth the first lesson said by a bored listener after a long speech or lecture or unwanted explanation. Since around 1870. From the phrase used in church at the end of a Bible reading.

here goes! said by somebody about to (try to) do something that is likely to be unsuccessful, or perhaps dangerous, as in *I'm not sure what'll happen when I switch it on, but here goes!* Since 1829 or earlier. See also **here we go!**

here we go! a variant of **here goes** or **here we go again!** In modern usage the phrase is also chanted repetitively by football supporters, lager louts, etc., to the tune of Sousa's march *The Stars and Stripes Forever*, as a general cry of (mutual) encouragement or aggression, often in the form *'ere we go, 'ere we go, 'ere we go!*

here we go again! we're in for a repetition of something unpleasant or undesirable; usually said in a tone of resigned despair, e.g. when somebody launches into an all-too-familiar complaint. Since around 1950 or earlier. See also **here we go!**

here's a couple of matchsticks jocularly addressed to one who seems to be having difficulty staying awake, e.g. at work. Late 19th–20th centuries. The implication is, of course, that the matchsticks may be used to prop open the would-be sleeper's eyelids.

here's another fine mess you've gotten me into! see **another fine mess you've gotten me into!**

hi ho, Silver(, away)! let's go!; off we go! A catch phrase of the radio series *The Lone Ranger*, first broadcast in the 1930s. The Lone Ranger was a masked rider who rode the plains of the Wild West on his horse Silver, with his faithful Indian companion Tonto, righting wrongs and enforcing law and order. The cry *hi ho* is variously transliterated as hi-*yo*, *hey ho*, *heigh ho*, etc.

hills are closing in on him, the he is beginning to go mad. The phrase was first used by United Nations troops in Korea in the early 1950s, referring to the forbidding hills and mountains of that country. A similar phrase, *the wire's closing in*, was used by Allied prisoners-of-war during World War II.

hint! hint! an accompaniment any hint that's about as subtle as a jab in the ribs, as in *there's a lovely pair of ear-rings in the jeweller's window – it's my birthday next week, hint, hint!* The phrase probably dates from around 1955.

hold me back! an expression of mock fury, the implication being that if you don't hold me back, I may hit somebody. Since 1915 or earlier. A coward or reluctant fighter may add the plea *well, go on, hold me!* A similar phrase is *wanna fight? I'll hold your coat*, used as a jocular way of defusing a situation that could come to blows.

hold onto your hat! we are about to embark on an exciting and possibly dangerous course of action. Used in the UK and the USA during the 20th century. From speeding in an open car or riding on a roller coaster.

hold your horses! just wait a minute; you're going too fast, or assuming too much. Since the mid-19th century or earlier.

home, James(, and don't spare the horses)! take me home; it's time to go home; let's go home. The full form of the phrase was popularized as the title of a song by Fred Hillebrand (1934), but probably

dates from around 1870 or earlier; the shortened form came into
general use around 1925. The phrase was originally addressed by a
man about town to his private coachman, then to his chauffeur; in
modern usage (since around 1945) it may be addressed to anybody
giving one a lift home by car, or to a friend, husband, wife, child,
etc., who is to travel home with the speaker. There is an amusing
example of usage in Catherine Aird's thriller *The Complete Steel*
(1969): 'Detective Constable Crosby turned the police car . . ..
"Home James, and don't spare the horses," commanded Sloan,
climbing in. "Beg pardon, sir?" Sloan sighed. "Headquarters, Crosby,
please." But then, the constable *was* a rather dull fellow.'

honest Injun!   honestly!; you can take my word for it. Used in the USA
since the early 1880s and in the UK from around 1895, popularized
by the books of Mark Twain, but obsolescent by the mid-20th
century. See also **scout's honour!**

horse of another (or **a different**) **colour, a**   see **that's a horse of another** (or **a different**) **colour.**

horses for courses   applied to what is appropriate in given circumstances. The phrase originated in horse-racing circles, perhaps as
early as 1860; around 1890 it began to be used in the upper classes
with reference to suitable marriages (as opposed to mésalliances).
The modern sense and usage of the phrase date from around 1945.

horses sweat, men perspire, (and or **but) ladies only glow**   a mild and
usually jocular reproof directed at a man who says that he (or a
woman) is sweating, or at a woman saying that she sweats or per-
spires. A catch phrase of the 20th century.

hot and strong   see **I like my women hot and strong.**

how about that!   an expression of surprise at what one has just been
told or at what one has found out. Used in the USA since the 1930s
and in the UK from the 1950s. The phrase is sometimes followed by
then, especially when commenting upon something surprising or
remarkable, as in the catch phrase of the British disc-jockey Jimmy
Savile: 'How's about that then, guys and gals?' See also **well, what do
you know!**

how can (or *could*) **you?**   how can (or could) you be so foolish, insensitive, etc.?; how can (or could) you bear to do or say that? Since
around 1910 or earlier.

how daft can you get?   a general comment on anything that is close to
the absolute limit of human folly or stupidity, as in *they're going to
scrap the whole system and start again: how daft can you get?* Since around
1930.

how does that grab you?   what do you think of that?; does that interest or excite you?, as in *we could stop off at the pub on the way home: how does that grab you?* Probably of US origin; used in the UK since the 1960s or earlier.

how goes the enemy? what's the time? A catch phrase of the 19th and early 20th centuries. It is a quotation from Frederick Reynolds' play *The Dramatist* (1789), spoken by 'Ennui the Timekiller, whose business in life is to murder the hour'. A variant of the phrase is *what says the enemy?*

how long is a piece of string? a trick question to which there is no possible answer; also used as a retort to a stupid or unanswerable question. Since around 1920 or earlier. It is sometimes extended to *how long is a piece of string when it's wet?* or *how long is a piece of string, and if so, why?* Similar phrases include *how high is up?* and *how high is a Chinaman?* (the latter containing a pun on How Hi, a fanciful Chinese name, attributed to the music-hall star Will Hay).

how many beans make five? a trick question or catch phrase. Since the late 19th century, when it was used in a music-hall song. Possible responses include 'six if you're a buyer, four if you're a seller' or 'two beans two half-beans one-and-a-half beans and half a bean' (said all in one breath). The idiom *to know how many beans make five* means 'to be shrewd, sensible, practical, worldly-wise, etc.'.

how many times? addressed to a newly married man, referring of course to the number of times he made love to his bride on their wedding night. Used in the USA since the 1890s or earlier, and subsequently in the UK.

how much? what did you say?; what do you mean? Since around 1845.

how much to get out? said facetiously to the person collecting the admission fee at the door for a jumble sale, charity show or similar function. Since around 1930.

how to win friends and influence people a business slogan used as a catch phrase, often derisively or ironically (e.g. as a comment on behaviour that is likely to have the opposite effect). It was popularized as the title of a book by Dale Carnegie, published in 1936, but the phrase had actually come into existence some years earlier.

how's that? see **'owzat!** (or **'owsat!**).

how's tricks? how are you?; how are things going? A friendly greeting. Used in the USA since the early 20th century and adopted in the UK by 1920.

how's your father? a catch phrase of the music-halls; often hyphenated and used as a noun, in the sense of 'sex', 'business', 'nonsense', etc., as in *a bit of how's-your-father behind the bicycle sheds*; *I can't be bothered with all that how's-your-father.*

how's your love life? addressed, for example, by a young man to a girl
   he hopes to get off with; also used as a general inquiry between
   friends, etc., often with sexual connotations. From around 1950.
howzat! (or **howsat!**)   see **'owzat!** (or **'owsat!**).
hubba! hubba! an expression of approval, addressed, for example, to
   an attractive young woman. Used in Australia since around 1930 and
   in the USA since the 1940s or earlier. The phrase may be derived
   from the same source as the noun *hubbub*, i.e. from a Gaelic cry.

I

I ask you! that's ridiculous, don't you think?; an expression of incredulous or derisive disapproval, intensifying the statement to which it is appended, as in *how do they expect us to believe that? I ask you! Climbing trees at his age! I ask you!* The phrase may be of French origin, possibly dating from the mid-1850s; it has been used in English throughout the 20th century.

I **believe you, (but) thousands wouldn't** an expression of disbelief, often implying, in a jocular way, that the addressee is a liar, as in *'It was an accident, honestly!' 'I believe you, thousands wouldn't.'* A catch phrase of the late 19th–20th centuries.

I bet you say that to all the girls a feminine response to a flattering or complimentary remark (especially one prompted by an ulterior motive); also used as a derisive counterattack. Since the mid-1920s or earlier.

I can take a hint (often preceded by *all right, OK,* etc.) an ironic response to a command or an unvarnished request to do something. Since the 1930s.

I can hardly wait ironically applied to an imminent and undesirable (or unexciting) occurrence, as in *'They've invited us round to watch a video of their holiday.' 'I can hardly wait.'* Since around 1930. In the UK, the phrase *I can't wait* is sometimes used instead, as in Noël Coward's *Present Laughter* (1943): '"She's coming to the station tomorrow morning to see us off – you don't mind, do you?" "I can't wait."'

I could care less a chiefly US variant of **I couldn't care less**, perhaps influenced by such phrases as **I should worry**.

I could eat that without salt a masculine remark applicable to an attractive girl or young woman who happens to pass by. The phrase has been used in this way since around 1945, but may be at least two centuries older – in Jonathan Swift's *Polite Conversation* (1738) occurs the line: 'But pray, my Lady Smart, does not Miss look as if she could eat me without salt?' See also **you look good enough to eat**.

I couldn't care less an expression of indifference, lack of interest or lack of concern, as in *'She won't be pleased.' 'I couldn't care less.'* Since around 1940. The phrase is also used with different subjects and in

different tenses, as in Sydney Moseley's *God Help America!* (1952):
'Ordinary citizens "couldn't have cared less!" – to use a cant post-war
phrase current in England.'

I didn't know you cared an ironic response to a critical or unpleasant
remark; also used in the same circumstances as **this is so sudden!**
Since around 1945. In the mid-1970s the phrase was used as the title
of a television comedy series by Peter Tinniswood.

I do not wish to know that see **I say, I say, I say!**

I don't mind if I do! yes, please!; an expression of enthusiastic acceptance, as in *'Won't you join us?' 'I don't mind if I do!'* The phrase probably
dates from around 1860 in this form; an earlier variant is *I don't care
if I do!* It was popularized by the UK radio series *ITMA* (first broadcast
in 1939), as the stock response of the character Colonel Chinstrap
to any remark that could be interpreted as an offer of a drink. The
phrase had been used in similar circumstances many years earlier,
in a *Punch* cartoon of 1880: '*Porter.* "Virginia Water!" *Bibulous old
gentleman* (seated in railway carriage): "Gin and water! I don't mind
if I do!"'

I **don't know!** elliptical for 'I don't know what to say (or think)!';
spoken in a tone of exasperation or shocked surprise, as in *really, I
don't know! Whatever will they think of next?* Late 19th–20th centuries.

I don't know much about art (or **music**, etc.), **but I know what I like**
a remark that ranks as number one in Gelett Burgess's list of
'bromides' (clichés or platitudes) in his witty monograph *Are You a
Bromide?* (1906). It probably dates from the late 19th century. The
phrase occurs in Max Beerbohm's *Zuleika Dobson* (1911): 'She was
one of the people who say "I don't know anything about music really,
but I know what I like."' Henry James used a similar phrase in his
novel *Portrait of a Lady* (1881): 'I don't care anything about reasons,
but I know what I like.' The variant *I don't know much about . . ., but
I know what I* don't *like* is also heard in modern usage.

I don't know whether I'm Arthur or Martha I don't know whether
I'm coming or going; used by men or women about themselves or
(with *he* or *she* in place of *I*) about anybody in a general state of
muddle. Used in Australia since the 1950s or earlier. In the USA, the
phrase *Arthur and Martha* sometimes has sexual overtones, used
especially by sado-masochistic homosexuals.

I don't mean maybe see **and I don't mean maybe**.

I *don't* think! reverses the preceding (usually ironic) statement or
remark, as in *very funny, I* don't *think!*; also used as an expression of
scepticism or disbelief, as in *she said it was an accident – I* don't *think!*
Since around 1880.

I don't wish to know that   see **I say, I say, I say!**

I feel like a mushroom: everyone keeps me in the dark and is always feeding me bullshit   a catch phrase of the 1970s-80s, of US origin. Similar sentiments were expressed in a catch phrase of the early 1940s: *I'm always out of the picture, just clambering round the frame.*

I forgot to duck   said, by way of explanation, by somebody with a black eye or similar injury. The phrase is traditionally associated with the US boxer Jack Dempsey, who said to his wife after losing the world heavyweight title in 1926: 'Honey, I just forgot to duck.' It also featured in a music-hall comedy sketch, and was repopularized in 1981 by the US president Ronald Reagan, after he was wounded in an assassination attempt.

I guess you're trying to tell me something   an ironic response to a point clearly made, as in *'Drop dead!' 'I guess you're trying to tell me something.'* Since around 1965. See also **are you trying to tell me something?**

I had 'em rolling in the aisles   said by a comedian who has succeeded in making the audience laugh uproariously. Since around 1920. Variants include *I had 'em in the aisles* and *I laid 'em in the aisles.* The phrase *rolling in the aisles* describes an audience that is helpless with laughter, as in *by the end of his act they were rolling in the aisles.*

I have my agents   I'm well informed in the matter; I have private sources of information; often used jocularly in reply to the question 'How did you know?' Since around 1939. Variants include *I have my spies* and *my spies are everywhere.*

I have to hand it to you   see **hand it to you, I have (or I've got) to.**

I have to see a man about a dog   see **see a man about a dog, I have (or I've got) to.**

I haven't got a thing to wear   a catch phrase generally used by women 'I haven't got a suitable outfit (for this special occasion) that I haven't worn at least once before'. The phrase dates from the 1890s or earlier; in modern usage it is often said in jocular self-parody.

I haven't laughed so much since my auntie caught her tit in the mangle   I haven't laughed so much for a long time; a reaction, for example, to the misfortune of somebody who is unpopular. A sick joke of the 20th century, current many years before sick humour became fashionable. Variants of the phrase substitute *mother* or *grandma* for *auntie,* and/or *left tit* or *tits* for *tit.* Nicholas Monserrat's *The Cruel Sea* (1951) contains the phrase '. . . since Ma caught her tits . . .'.

I hear what you say   I don't accept or agree with what you have just said in full, but I take your point. (A variant substitutes *note* for *hear.*) The phrase may be an elaboration of *I hear you,* meaning 'the remark you have just made is untrue or not worth answering', which is of

Scottish origin and dates from around 1905. (In US usage *I hear you* means 'I understand', which is gaining currency in the UK in the 1990s.)

I hope I'm not interrupting anything   said, for example, by one who enters a room and finds a couple kissing or embracing, or in any apparently compromising situation. Since the 1920s. *I hope I don't intrude* is an earlier form of the phrase, dating back to the 19th century.

I kid you not   I mean it; I'm being serious; I'm telling the truth. It was popularized by the film *The Caine Mutiny* (1954), based on the best-selling novel of the same name by Herman Wouk (1951), in which this phrase is the trademark of the character Captain Queeg (played by Humphrey Bogart in the film).

I *like* it!   an expression of approbation or amusement. The phrase may have originated in the armed forces; it has been in civilian usage since around 1960.

I like my women hot and strong   derived from the phrase 'I like my coffee – and my women – hot and strong' or some variant thereof. Since around 1945. Variants of the phrase replace *hot and strong* with *hot, black and strong*, or *I like my* with *he likes his*. The phrase may also be used by or of women, in the form *I like my men . . .* or *she likes her men . . ..*

I like that! (, well)   an ironic exclamation of indignation, especially in response to something that is unjust, untrue, ungrateful, impudent, etc., as in *'She said you threw her out.' 'I like that! I begged her to stay!'*; *Well, I like that! We've been standing here for ages, and he just strolls to the front of the queue and gets served!* Late 19th–20th centuries.

I like work: I could watch it all day   a catch phrase derived from a passage in Jerome K. Jerome's *Three Men in Boat* (1889): 'I like work; it fascinates me. I can sit and look at it for hours. I love to keep it by me; the idea of getting rid of it nearly breaks my heart.'

I like your nerve!   see **of all the nerve!**

I love you too   an ironic response to an insult, or to any remark unpleasant enough to demand a reply but not worth picking a fight over. Used in the USA since around 1960 and subsequently adopted in the UK.

I must go and shake hands with the wife's best friend   see **shake hands with the wife's best friend, I must go and**.

I must love you and leave you   sorry, I must go; a jocular or polite valediction used among friends, acquaintances, etc. From around 1880 or earlier. The full form of the phrase has the ending *. . ., as sailors do their wives*. Variants include *I must love and leave you* and *I'll* *love you and leave you.* See also **fuck 'em and chuck 'em**.

I need that like (I need) a hole in the head I don't need it all. The phrase usually refers to something that is at best undesirable and would at worst be disastrous. Adopted from the USA around 1950.

I never liked it, anyway! applied to something broken, lost, etc., said in a tone of mock resignation or with a philosophical shrug of the shoulders. Since the late 1940s.

I note what you say see **I hear what you say**.

I only asked (with heavy emphasis on *asked*, pronounced *arsked*) said in hurt tones when somebody responds snappishly to a question or remark. The phrase was popularized by Bernard Bresslaw, as the gormless private 'Popeye' Popplewell, in the UK television series *The Army Game* (first broadcast in 1957).

I only do it for kicks I wouldn't do it at all if I didn't get a thrill out of it. Used in the USA since the 1920s and in the UK from the 1950s. Other personal pronouns may be substituted for *I*, as in *he doesn't need the money – he only does it for kicks*.

I only work here I am not responsible for my employer's policy or methods; often preceded by *don't blame me, . . ., I don't make the rules, . . .*, etc. Since the late 1940s. See also **don't ask *me*, I only live** (or **work) here**.

I owe you one I am very much obliged to you; also used as a threat of retaliation. The phrase occurs in George Colman the Younger's play *The Poor Gentleman: A Comedy* (1802), in response to a witticism: 'Come, that's very well, indeed! Thank you, good sir – I owe you one!' It may be elliptical for 'I owe you a drink for that'.

I say, I say, I say! a catch phrase that originated in the music-hall, used to introduce a corny question-and-answer joke, usually by one comic interrupting another. Since the 1890s or earlier; still occasionally used in comedy shows. The traditional response to a joke introduced by *I say, . . .!* is *I don't* (or *do not*) *wish to know that – kindly leave the stage!* This phrase is sometimes used in other circumstances (with or without *kindly leave the stage!*), e.g. in response to an irrelevant remark, or one that causes annoyance, disgust, envy, etc.

I see, said the blind man said by one who understands, but not fully, or by one who doesn't understand at all. Used in the USA since around 1860 and subsequently adopted in the UK. Extensions of the phrase include *. . ., when he couldn't see at all* and the punning *. . ., as he picked up his hammer and saw.*

I shan't play! said peevishly (or with mock peevishness) by a child who is annoyed or upset; also said jocularly by adults. Used in Australia since around 1885; also used in the UK. Variants include *shan't play!*

and *I'm not playing!*, as in *this isn't fair – I'm not playing!*

I should be so lucky!   expresses philosophical or cheerful acceptance of the improbability of such good fortune; virtually synonymous with **some hope!**   The phrase is also used ironically or jocularly in response to a warning, as in *'He might leave you.' 'I should be so lucky!'*; *'She's a gold-digger – she'll suck you dry.' 'I should be so lucky!'* (said with sexual innuendo). Of Yiddish origin, the phrase has been used in the USA from around 1930 and in the UK since around 1960 or earlier. Other personal pronouns, especially *you*, may be substituted for *I*; the phrase *you should be so lucky!* is often derisive.

I should cocoa!   I should say so!; an expression of emphatic agreement, more frequently used ironically to express disagreement, derision, indignation, disbelief, etc. The phrase originated in Cockney rhyming slang of the 20th century.

I should live so long!   I'll be very lucky indeed if I'm still alive when that happens (usually referring to something that is unlikely to happen in the near future, if ever). A Yiddish catch phrase dating from around 1920 or earlier.

I should worry!   I don't care; an expression of indifference or lack of concern. The phrase occurs in Jack Ripley's *Davis Doesn't Live Here Any More* (1971): 'I should worry! I have already broken so many rules, an extra breakage will go unnoticed.' Of Yiddish origin, the phrase has been used in the USA since the early 20th century and was subsequently adopted in the UK.

I tell you what!   see **I'll tell you what!**

I thought you'd never ask!   see **thought you'd never ask!**

I took my harp to the party, but nobody asked me to play   said by one who goes prepared to do something but is not given the opportunity to do it. The phrase comes from a popular song by Desmond Carter and Noël Gay, made famous by Gracie Fields in the early 1930s.

I want it yesterday   I want it immediately, if not sooner. Used in the USA since the 1940s; also used in the UK. Other pronouns (or nouns) may be substituted for *I*, referring to the often needless impatience of a person, organization, etc.

I washed my hair last night and now I can't do a thing with it   a genuine or jocular lament, or an excuse for untidy or uncontrollable hair; the second half of the phrase is often said in chorus as a response to the opening statement. The phrase may have originated in the world of entertainment.

I wasn't born yesterday   I'm not a fool; said, for example, in response to an attempt to cheat or deceive the speaker. Late 19th–20th centuries.

I wouldn't be seen dead in it   applied to an unfashionable or otherwise unattractive article of clothing (perhaps echoing the principle that you should always wear clean underwear 'in case you get knocked down by a bus'). A catch phrase of the 20th century used more by women than men. A less frequent variant substitutes the more logical (and perhaps original) *found* for *seen*.

I wouldn't believe him (or **her**, etc.) **on a stack of Bibles**   he (or she, etc.) is a liar. Used in the USA since the 1930s or earlier; also used in the UK.

I wouldn't bet on it!   you would be foolishly rash to count on it; it is unlikely to happen. The phrase has been in general use since the late 19th century; by the mid-20th century it had become a cliché. A variant is *don't bet on it!*

I wouldn't kick *her* out of bed   the response of a certain type of male on seeing (a photograph of) an attractive female. Since around 1920. Without the stress on *her*, the phrase means 'she's no beauty, but...'. Less frequent variants include *I wouldn't climb over* her *to get at* you*!* and *I'd rather sleep with her with no clothes on than with you in your best suit.* Also used more recently by women with '*him*'.

I wouldn't know!   I don't know; often said with the nuance 'I'm in no position to know', 'I can't be expected to know', 'I don't know because nobody has seen fit to tell me' or 'I don't know and I don't care'. It may also imply that the matter in question is outside the speaker's territory: a proud claim to ignorance of a subject that doesn't interest one. The phrase probably originated in the USA around 1925 and was adopted in the UK in the late 1930s.

I wouldn't know him from a bar of soap   I don't know him; I wouldn't recognize him if I saw him; an Australian variant of the phrase *I wouldn't know him from Adam.* Probably since around 1910. The pronoun *him* may, of course, be replaced by *her*; another Australian variant substitutes *crow* for *bar of soap*.

I wouldn't like to meet him (or **her**) **in the dark**   applied to any man or woman of formidable, dangerous or sinister appearance or character. A catch phrase of the 20th century. Variants of the phrase substitute *in a dark alley* or *on a dark night* for *in the dark*.

I wouldn't piss on him (or **her**) **if he was on fire**   an expression of extreme dislike. Chiefly used in Australia in the later 20th century, but probably of British origin.

I wouldn't say no!   yes, please!, as in *'Would you like a drink?' 'I wouldn't say no!'* The phrase has been used in this way since around 1920.

I wouldn't trust him (or **her**) **as far as I could throw him** (or **her**)   applied to a spectacularly untrustworthy person. From around 1870.

Variants of the phrase include . . . *as far as I could throw an anvil in a swamp,* . . . *throw a piano* and . . . *throw a pregnant elephant.* There is also the rider . . . *and I wouldn't bother to pick him* (or *her*) *up.*

I wouldn't want to be a pawnbroker's sign on a night like this   see **cold enough to freeze the balls off a brass monkey.**

I'd love to be a fly on the wall   I should very much like to see and hear what is going on (at a specified place, event, meeting, discussion, etc.) without being noticed. A catch phrase of the 20th century. It has given rise to the attributive phrase *fly-on-the-wall,* as in *a fly-on-the-wall documentary.*

I'd rather sleep with her with no clothes on than with you in your best suit   see **I wouldn't kick** *her* **out of bed.**

I'll cut you off with (or **without**) **a shilling**   see **I'll strike you out of my will.**

I'll drink to that!   an expression of hearty assent or agreement. Probably of US origin, from around 1950; also used in the UK. It was further popularized by the US television series *Rowan and Martin's Laugh-In* (first broadcast in 1967, also in the UK).

I'll eat my hat!   an expression of surprise at something that has happened. A catch phrase of the late 19th–20th centuries. The cliché *if . . ., I'll eat my hat* refers to something that is unlikely to happen.

I'll expect you when I see you   addressed to one who is unable to give a reliable estimate of his or her time of arrival. The phrase also occurs in the form *expect me when you see me,* said by one who has little or no idea what time he or she will arrive. Late 19th–20th centuries; originally applied to somebody whose announcement of a visit or meeting is not to be depended upon.

I'll go out into the garden and eat worms   I'll eat humble pie; often used ironically. Probably since around 1880. The phrase is also used in the sense in which it occurs in the children's song that begins: 'Nobody loves me, everybody hates me, / I'm going to the garden to eat worms.'

I'll hate myself in the morning   a jocular way of declining a sexual (or other) proposition; also said by one purchasing or consuming that last drink of the evening which will inevitably produce a horrible hangover. From the earlier mother-to-daughter or woman-to-woman catch phrase *you'll hate yourself in the morning,* recommending chastity.

I'll have your guts for garters!   a threat (originally serious, but usually jocular in modern usage). Other words may be substituted for *I* and/or *your,* as in *the boss will have my guts for garters* and the following quotation from Desmond Bagley's *Landslide* (1967): 'Your father isn't going to like that. He'll have your guts for garters.' The phrase dates back to the 18th century or earlier; Robert Greene's *James the Fourth* (1598) contains the line: 'I'll make garters of thy guts, thou villain.'

I'll let you off this time originally an adult's monitory condonation of a child's misdemeanour, now used jocularly by people of all ages to excuse some stupidity of their own (usually brought to their attention by the person addressed). Since around 1950.

I'll love you and leave you see **I must love you and leave you**.

I'll say! an expression of enthusiastic agreement; elliptical for 'I'll say it is!' or 'I'll say so!', as in *'Pretty impressive, isn't it?' 'I'll say!'* Adopted from the USA around 1925.

I'll see you in court! see **see you in court!**

I'll see you in hell first a vehement refusal or a response to a challenge. The phrase dates from the late 19th century or earlier. Variants include *I'll see you damned* (or *hanged*) *first.*

I'll show you mine if you'll show me yours a jocular response to any request to show somebody something, used in imitation of children comparing their genitals, as in Frederick Forsyth's *The Dogs of War* (1974): '"Have you any scars from wounds? . . . Show me," she said. . . . "I'll show you mine, if you'll show me yours," he taunted, mimicking the old kindergarten challenge.' The phrase probably dates back to the 19th century or earlier.

I'll strike you out of my will used jocularly among those who have little or nothing to leave. Since the mid-1940s or earlier. Variants include *I'll cut you off with* (or *without*) *a shilling.*

I'll take a rain-check I'll accept (your invitation, etc.) another time or at a later date, if I may. Used in the US since the late 1940s and in the UK from around 1970. A *rain-check* is a ticket, or the stub of a ticket, valid for the replay of a game cancelled or abandoned because of bad weather.

I'll tell you one thing, and that's not (or **that ain't**) **two** used to emphasize the statement that follows. Since the 18th century in the form . . . *that's not two,* and since the 19th century in the form . . . *that ain't two.*

I'll tell you what! introduces a proposal or suggestion, as in *I'll tell you what – let's pretend we don't recognize him!* Since the 17th century; in modern usage the phrase is often shortened to *I tell you what!* or *tell you what!*

I'll try anything once said by the adventurous and the experimental, with reference to food, drink, sexual activities, leisure pursuits, etc. Since around 1925. The phrase is sometimes extended, as in *I'll try* *anything once, except sodomy and British sherry* (or *pasteurized beer, processed cheese*, etc.).

I'm a big girl (or **boy**) **now**   see **you're a big girl** (or **boy**) **now.**

I'm a devout coward   see **it's against my religion.**

I'm a stranger here myself   used as a general excuse for inability or unwillingness to help, as in Dorothy Halliday's *Dolly and the Cookie Bird* (1970): "'I suppose you don't know where he's hidden the rubies?' 'I'm a stranger here myself.'" The phrase has been used in this way since around 1950. From the standard response received when one stranger asks another for directions.

I'm all right, Jack   see **fuck you, Jack, I'm all right.**

I'm from Missouri(, you('ll) have to show me)   said by one who is extremely sceptical, or extremely reluctant to believe without proof. A US catch phrase that may date back to the 19th century. 'I'm from Missouri and You've Got to Show Me' is the title of a song by Lee Raney and Ned Wayburn.

I'm not just a pretty face(, you know)   I do possess some intelligence; I do have other abilities, qualities, etc.; often said with pride or triumph after proving this point, especially by a woman but also, jocularly, by men. The rejoinder 'not *even* a pretty face' is sometimes heard. Other pronouns may be used in place of *I*, as in *she's not just a pretty face – she's a dab hand at fixing cars; well done – you're not just a pretty face, are you?* Since around 1965 or earlier.

I'm not playing!   see **I shan't play!**

I'm not as (or **so**) **green as I'm cabbage-looking**   see **not as** (or **so**) **green as I'm cabbage-looking, I'm.**

I'm not that kind of girl   originally a feminine response to a sexual proposition, subsequently used as a jocular reply to any mildly dubious proposal. The phrase may date from around 1880.

I'm only here for the beer   see **only here for the beer.**

I've been there   I have experience of whatever is under discussion; also used as a boast of worldly wisdom or sexual experience. Adopted from the USA around 1900.

I've got news for you!   I have something important or startling to tell you, or something that contradicts what you have just said. Since the late 1940s or early 1950s. In the 1970s the phrase was adapted by the *Daily Mail* as an advertising slogan: 'We have news for you.' See also **have I got news for you!**

I've got the time if you've got the inclination   a jocular response to the question 'Have you got the time?', meaning 'What time is it?' Variants include *yes, but not the inclination* and *yes, if you've got the money*. The phrase (and its variant *I've got the time if you've got the money*) alludes to the services of a prostitute (or enthusiastic amateur). Since around 1950 it has also been used as a jocular response to such exclamations as 'bugger me!' or 'fuck me!'

I've got to hand it to you see **hand it to you, I have** (or **I've got**) **to.**

I've got to see a man about a dog see **see a man about a dog, I have** (or **I've got**) **to.**

I've had more women than you've had hot dinners (or **breakfasts**) an older man's cynically jocular boast to a younger, less experienced man. The counterpart substitutes *men* for *women*. A catch phrase of the 20th century. It is also used in non-sexual contexts, with other phrases in place of *I've had more women*, as in *she's written more books than you've had hot dinners.*

I've had my moments my achievements may not be conspicuous, but they are at least as substantial as those of others (who choose to boast about theirs), as in *you may think I'm a boring old fart, but I've had my moments!* The phrase probably originated in the UK before 1940. It may refer to sexual satisfaction, or (especially since around 1965) to any other 'moments' of excitement or success. In sexual contexts the variant *I've had my ups and downs* is sometimes used in its place. See also **we all have our moments.**

I've started, so I'll finish a catch phrase of the UK television quiz show *Mastermind* (first broadcast in 1972). It is said by Magnus Magnusson, the question-master, when the time signal interrupts a question he is posing to a 'contender'. The phrase is used jocularly by the general public in any appropriate situation, sometimes with a double meaning.

if all else fails, read the instructions! said to or by somebody who has plunged straight into trying to do something (e.g. assemble or operate an unfamiliar device) without giving the matter careful thought first, and has failed. Later 20th century. A variant of the phrase has *when* in place of *if.*

if, and it's a big if introduces a very improbable supposition or hypothesis. 20th century. The phrase *it's a big if* is sometimes used alone, by one who pours cold water on another's supposition or hypothesis, as in *'If we win, . . .' 'It's a big if.'*

if anything can go wrong, it will see **anything that *can* go wrong *will* go wrong.**

if he doesn't like it he may do the other thing! see **if you don't like it you can lump it!**

if he fell in the shit he'd come up smelling of violets (or **roses**) applied to somebody who is extraordinarily lucky on a specific occasion, especially one who habitually enjoys such good fortune. Other personal pronouns may be used in place of *he*, and there are numerous variants, such as *he could fall into a cart of shit and come out with a gold watch* or *if he fell in the river he'd only get dusty*. The original phrase has given rise to the idiom *to come up smelling of roses*, meaning 'to emerge untarnished from a sticky situation'.

if it's Tuesday, it must be Belgium   jocularly applied to very fast tours in which a different country or place of interest is 'done' each day. The phrase comes from the title of a US comedy film, *If It's Tuesday, This Must Be Belgium* (1969); in general usage other days of the week and place-names may be substituted for *Tuesday* and *Belgium*. The phrase is also used in other situations (e.g. a crash training-course) where the speed of progress or the pace of activity causes general confusion.

if the wind changes, you'll get stuck like that   said to a child making a silly face, grimacing, pouting, squinting, etc.; also used jocularly among adults. The phrase has been part of domestic folklore since the beginning of the 20th century, and probably much earlier.

if you can't beat 'em, join 'em   originally used in political contexts, now said in any appropriate situation, e.g. when giving up a struggle against more successful rivals and following their example instead. The phrase may have originated in the US (with *lick* in place of *beat*); it has been used in the UK since the early 1940s.

if you can't fight, wear a big 'at   a taunt directed at somebody wearing a new hat, or at a soldier in best uniform. The phrase dates from the 1930s or earlier in Cockney usage.

if you can't stand the heat, get out of the kitchen   if you can't cope with the pace, strain, etc., of a situation, leave it to those who can. Used in the USA from around 1950 and adopted in the UK around 1970. The phrase is traditionally attributed to the US president Harry S Truman, who frequently used it; however, it was probably originated by a member of his military staff, Harry Vaughan.

if you don't like it you can lump it!   if you don't like it, you'll just have to put up with it. Since around 1860 or earlier. The phrase has the variant *if you don't like it you may do the other thing* (or **you know what you can do with it**), which may also be a euphemistic reference to the more vulgar variant *if you don't like it, you can stick* (or *shove*, etc.) *it up your arse* (see also **put it where the monkey put the nuts**). In all these phrases other personal pronouns may be substituted for *you*, as in *if he doesn't like it he may do the other thing!*

if you knows of a better 'ole(, go to it)!(, well,)   a catch phrase that originated as the caption of a cartoon by Captain Bruce Bairnsfather, printed in *Fragments of France* (1915).

if you say so I don't agree with you (or believe you), but I'm not going to argue the point; also said by one who (grudgingly) accepts another's opinion, assertion, etc. Used as a catch phrase since around 1950 or earlier.

if you want to get ahead, get a hat! a catch phrase that probably originated in the 1930s, as an advertising slogan used by hatters or the Hat Council. It owes much of its popularity to the neat pun.

ignorance is bliss applied to any display of ignorance, in any sense of the word; also said by or of one who is in a state of ignorance. The catch phrase is used in a far wider range of situations than the context of the original quotation, from Thomas Gray's *Ode on a Distant Prospect of Eton College* (published in 1747): 'Where ignorance is bliss, / 'Tis folly to be wise.'

illegal, immoral or fattening refers to forbidden pleasures, especially in such phrases as *everything I like is either illegal, immoral or fattening; it's always the same: anything you like is either illegal, immoral, or fattening.* Used in the UK since around 1940. The phrase is attributed to the US writer Alexander Woollcott in the form: 'All the things I really like to do are either immoral, illegal, or fattening.'

illegitimis non carborundum a mock-Latin phrase meaning 'don't let the bastards grind you down (i.e. break your spirit)'. Carborundum (silicon carbide) is an extremely hard substance used in grinding and polishing. The phrase originated in the armed forces during World War II. Variants include *nil carborundum* (a pun on the Latin phrase *nil desperandum*, meaning 'never say die!'), which was used as the title of a play by Henry Livings (1962). The variant *Nolite te bastardes carborundorum* took on a sinister significance in Margaret Atwood's dystopian novel *The Handmaid's Tale (1985)*.

impossible we do at once; miracles take a little longer, the see **difficult we do at once; the impossible will take a little longer, the**.

in a while, crocodile see **see you later, alligator!**

in like Flynn(, he's) he's an easy winner; he's sitting pretty; a US catch phrase of the 20th century. The phrase is also used in Australia, where it is applied to one who seizes an opportunity, especially a sexual opportunity. The true identity of Flynn is uncertain: in US usage it may be Ed Flynn, whose Democratic Party machine exercised absolute political control over the Bronx, New York City; in Australian usage it is said to be the actor Errol Flynn, renowned for his sexual prowess. On the other hand, the name could have been chosen simply because it rhymes with *in*.

in spades a general intensifier, as in *you can say that in spades!; he's a bastard in spades; she did it – in spades!* Since around 1945. From card games in which spades is the top suit.

in the big league   describes somebody who is either rather grand, or full of self-importance. Since around 1920.

in the same ball-park   very approximately correct; also applied to a financial offer, estimate, guess, etc., that is not really very close. Used in the USA, possibly since the 1940s, and subsequently adopted in the UK. The phrase originated in baseball, referring to a hit that is far from getting the ball to the desired place, but at least it remains in the ball-park (i.e. the stadium). It often occurs in the negative form *not in the same ball-park*, and has given rise to the phrase *ball-park figures*, meaning 'rough estimate (of money, materials, etc., needed for a project)'.

in the wrong business, I'm (or **we're, you're**, etc.)   a ruefully jocular comment upon those who earn more for less work, or who make exorbitant charges or profits, as in *it only took them a couple of hours, and they sent me a bill for £500 – I think I'm in the wrong business!* Since the 1950s. A variant has *racket* in place of *business*.

include me out!   leave me out (of the discussion, plan, etc.). Used in the USA since the late 1940s and in the UK by 1950. The phrase is attributed to the US film producer Sam Goldwyn, and is believed to be one of the few genuine Goldwynisms.

is everybody happy?   is everybody satisfied, comfortable, etc.? The traditional hearty cry of a comedian trying to boost audience participation. The phrase may have originated in pantomime or vaudeville in the early 20th century; it was subsequently used in holiday camps, on radio programmes, etc. It is often associated with the US entertainer Ted Lewis, who made it his trademark; he also used it in the title of a popular song (1927) and starred in a film of the same name (1929).

is he (or **she**) **with you? – no, I thought he was** (or **she**) **with you!**   an exchange between two companions about a third, who has just made an exhibition of himself or herself, e.g. by breaking wind, making an embarrassing remark, etc. (Such behaviour is not, of course, restricted to the male sex: *she* may be substituted for *he*.) Since around 1950. See also **excuse my pig: he's a friend!**; **you can't take him** (or **her**) **anywhere!**

is my face red!   an exclamation of acute embarrassment. Adopted from the USA in the early 1950s. The phrase is also used in other tenses and with other personal pronouns, e.g. when recounting a moment of embarrassment, as in *was my* (or *his, her,* etc.) *face red!*

is that a threat or a promise?   a stock reply to any appropriate threat, promise or other proposition, as in *'I'll phone you every day.' 'Is that a* *threat or a promise?'* The phrase is often used with sexual innuendo, as in *'I'll see to you in five minutes' 'Is that a threat or a promise?'* Since the early 20th century. See also **promises, promises!**

is that all? an ironic or sarcastic response to an exorbitant price, a long list of duties, an unreasonable request, etc., as in *'They cost £500 each.' 'Oh, is that all? Let's have two!'* A catch phrase of the 20th century.

is that good? a question intended to disconcert one's interlocutor by its unexpectedness, as in *'I won a hundred pounds on the Derby!' 'Is that good?'* Probably since the early 20th century.

is the Pope Catholic? said in response to a stupid question. Of US origin, adopted in the UK around 1950 or earlier. The phrase is sometimes used in combination with **does a bear shit in the woods?** in the variant form *is a bear Catholic – does the Pope shit in the woods?*

is there a doctor in the house? the traditional cry heard when somebody is taken ill or has an accident in a theatre, cinema, etc.; used jocularly as a catch phrase since the late 1950s. It may have been popularized by Richard Gordon's novel *Doctor in the House* (1952), filmed in 1953.

is there a law against it? why shouldn't I? Used in response to a re-quest that the speaker considers unreasonable. Since around 1950.

is there room for a little one? addressed humbly or hopefully to the occupants of a crowded vehicle, seat, etc.; often used ironically, when the speaker is anything but small. A catch phrase of the 20th century.

is you is or is you ain't? are you or aren't you (sure, ready, in favour, etc.)? Originally used by US Blacks in the mid-1940s, the phrase comes from the popular song *Is You Is or Is You Ain't My Baby* (recorded in 1943). In the 1980s the song was used in a series of advertisements in the UK by a credit card company: *Does you does or does you don't take Access.*

isn't he (or **she**) **the lucky one!** see **lucky one!, aren't you** (or **I**) **the.**

isn't that just like a man (or **woman**)! applied to any display of the crassness, unpredictability, etc., that is considered typical of the opposite sex. Similar phrases include *you know what men are!* and *you know how women are!* Possibly since around 1850.

isn't that something? (or !) isn't that remarkable?!; an expression of emphatic admiration. Adopted from the USA around 1945.

it adds up see **it doesn't add up.**

it all depends (on) what you mean a temporizing catch phrase, used jocularly or derisively. The phrase was popularized by 'Professor' C. E. M. Joad on the UK radio programme *The Brains Trust* (first broadcast in 1941), in which a panel of experts answered questions sent in by the general public. Joad's replies inevitably began with the phrase *it all depends what you mean by . . .*, as in the example quoted by Nigel Rees in the *Bloomsbury Dictionary of Popular Phrases*: '"Are thoughts things or about things?" . . . "It all depends what you mean by a 'thing'."'

it beats working   see **beats working**.

it come off in me 'and   an excuse made by one who accidentally breaks something. Originally a domestic servants' catch phrase, dating from the mid-19th century or earlier. A variant is *it come to pieces in me 'ands.*

it couldn't happen (or **have happened**) **to a nicer chap** (or **guy**)   said to or of somebody who has received a well-deserved stroke of good fortune. Since the 1940s. In British usage (with *chap*) the phrase is usually sincere and genuinely congratulatory; in US usage (with *guy*) it is often ironic, referring to a well-deserved misfortune.

it didn't strike on my box   it left me indifferent; it didn't make a good impression. Since around 1960; now obsolescent. The phrase alludes to safety matches.

it doesn't add up   it doesn't make sense; perhaps elliptical for 'it doesn't add up correctly'. Used as a catch phrase since the late 1950s. It is the negative form of *it* (or *that*) *adds up*, a chiefly British variant of the US phrase *it* (or *that*) *figures*.

it doesn't stand up   said of a plan or scheme that has nothing to commend it, that is unlikely to be accepted, etc. Since around 1940. See also **it'll never get off the ground**.

it fell off the back of a lorry   applied to stolen goods offered for sale on street corners, in public-houses, etc. It is also used ironically to account for the possession of valuable, obviously stolen, property. Since around 1950. The phrase has other forms, such as the question *did it fall* (or *drop*) *off a lorry?*, posed by a prospective purchaser of such goods.

it fits where it touches   jocularly applied to loose, very ill-fitting clothes. Late 19th–20th centuries. For trousers, the plural form *they fit where they touch* is used; since around 1960 this phrase has also been applied to suggestively tight trousers.

it had my name (or **number**) **on it**   applied by a soldier to the bullet that wounded him. A catch phrase of World War I, revived in World War II. From the fatalistic theory expressed in the phrase *there's a bullet with my name on it*, said by a soldier who believes he will be killed or wounded in action, but until this bullet comes his way no other bullet will hit him.

it happens in the best-regulated (or **best of**) **families**   refers to any mishap or misdemeanour, especially (in British usage) the pregnancy of an unmarried member of the family. Since the mid-19th century or earlier. From the proverb *accidents will happen in the best-regulated families.*

it just goes to show a remark often made about something that does nothing of the sort. As a cliché, the phrase is usually uttered by one presented with proof or a demonstration of something surprising or unexpected, as in *it just goes to show – you can't trust anybody these days!* The phrase has been in use throughout the 20th century; since the 1930s it is sometimes jocularly altered to *it just shows to go.*

it looks like a wet weekend see **looks like a wet weekend**.

it must have been something he (or **she**) **ate** said by someone who attempts to account for another's health or mood. Since around 1950. There is a reference to this phrase in Michael Flanders and Donald Swann's song *The Reluctant Cannibal*: 'It must have been someone he ate.'

it seemed like a good idea at the time a limp excuse for a foolish action; applied in retrospect, jocularly or ruefully, to anything done impulsively or impetuously with disastrous consequences, whether or not these were foreseeable at the moment of action. Possibly since the 1930s or earlier.

it shouldn't happen to a dog! it's too unjust or unpleasant to be wished on a dog, let alone a human being! Since the 1930s; possibly of Yiddish origin. The British writer James Herriot adapted the phrase for the title of his book *It Shouldn't Happen to a Vet* (1972). A variant substitutes *that* for *it*, as in Terence Rattigan's play *Variations on a Theme* (1958): '"The last doctor's put her on a very strict régime. He even says she might have to . . . go to Switzerland . . . .." "Switzerland? That shouldn't happen to a dog."' See also **it's a dog's life**.

it stinks a term of extreme disapproval; applied to anything that offends one's intelligence, honesty, sense of taste, etc., as in *'What do you think of my idea?' 'It stinks.'* Adopted from the USA around 1945. See also **it sucks**.

it sucks a variant of **it stinks**. The phrase was particularly popular in the 1960s and the early 1970s, when it was used by students, musicians, drug addicts, etc.

it takes all sorts a comment upon the peculiarities of others; a truncated form of the proverb *it takes all sorts to make a world*, used as a catch phrase since the late 19th century. It occurs in Peter Driscoll's novel *The White Lie Assignment* (1971): 'I paid the driver and he swung away, shaking his head. It takes all sorts, he'd be thinking, and I suppose it does.'

it takes one to know one   you're as bad as the person you're criticizing, as in *'She's a liar.' 'It takes one to know one.'* Possibly since the mid-19th century. The phrase may be based on the proverbial principle of 'set a thief to catch a thief'.

it takes two to tango   sexual intercourse requires cooperation between the participants; usually said when one of those involved in an illicit liaison, an unwanted pregnancy, the procreation of a large family, etc., receives more than his or her fair share of the blame. Used in the USA since the early 1920s and subsequently adopted in the UK. The phrase is also applied to other activities, such as bribery, in which one party is no more or less guilty than the other.

it was close, but no cigar   see **close, but no cigar**.

it was on for young and old   refers to a general outburst of high spirits, whether innocuous or obnoxious, often with an implication of widespread agreement. Used in Australia since the mid-1940s.

it went down like a lead balloon   see **went down like a lead balloon, it** (or **that**).

it went like a bomb   it was a tremendous success, as in *the party went like a bomb*. (Note that this is the opposite of the chiefly US theatrical phrase *it bombed*, meaning 'it was a total failure'.) Since the late 1950s. The phrase *to go like a bomb* was originally applied (in the late 1940s) to cars with extremely rapid acceleration and a high top speed.

it would be cheap at half the price   see **cheap at half the price**.

it would make a cat laugh   see **enough to make a cat laugh**.

it'll all be the same in a hundred years   why worry?; a consolatory catch phrase. It is a variant of the proverb *it will all be the same a hundred years hence*, which has existed in one form or another since the 17th century or earlier. Jonathan Swift's *Polite Conversation* (1738) contains the phrase: ''twill all be one a thousand years hence'.

it'll all come out in the wash   it'll all be discovered eventually; now chiefly used in the sense of 'it'll all be settled eventually' or simply 'never mind (or don't worry) – it doesn't matter'. A catch phrase of the 20th century. A similar phrase is *it'll all rub off when it's dry*, applied to harsh words or summary punishment, which dates from the early 19th century.

it'll be a cold day in hell (when . . .)   refers to something that will never happen, or that is very unlikely to happen. Since the early 20th century. See also **that'll be the day**.

it'll be all right on the night   an expression of optimism applied to things that go wrong, but are expected subsequently to go right. In its original theatrical usage, referring to the first or opening night preceded by a (very) bad dress rehearsal, the phrase dates from around 1870; it has been in more general usage since around 1920. Since the late 1970s it has been used as the title of a series of UK television compilations of bloomers and out-takes, *It'll Be Alright on the Night*, presented by Denis Norden.

it'll never get off the ground applied to a plan or experiment that is unlikely to be accepted, that is bound to fail, etc. Since around 1942. An allusion to prototype aircraft that don't achieve flight. See also **it doesn't stand up**.

it'll put hair on your chest it will make you more virile, potent, etc.; chiefly applied to food or drink, especially strong liquor, as in *try this – it'll put hair on your chest!* The phrase is also used as a general invitation or encouragement to drink. Late 19th–20th centuries. See also **that'll put lead in your pencil**.

it'll see me out it'll last my time. The phrase is perhaps more frequently used in the form *it'll see you out*.

it's a bastard applied to anything that is very difficult or extremely exasperating. 20th century. Variants include *it's a bugger, it's a sod*, etc.

it's a big if see *if*, and it's a big if.

it's a breeze a variant of **it's a piece of cake**. Used in the USA and Australia since before 1945; also used in the UK. The phrase may be derived from sailing. See also **it's a doddle**.

it's a cinch see **cinch, it's** (or **that's**) **a**.

it's a different (or **whole new**) **ball game** see **ball game, it's a different** (or **whole new**).

it's a doddle a variant of **it's a piece of cake**. Used by the British armed forces since around 1945 and by civilians from 1950. See also **it's a breeze**.

it's a dog's life applied to any unpleasant or undesirable situation, job, way of life, etc. The phrase is also used ironically in the opposite sense, referring to a life of ease. It is probably derived from the 17th-century proverb *a dog's life, hunger and ease*. See also **it shouldn't happen to a dog!**

it's a fair cop a catch phrase traditionally addressed to a police officer by a petty thief, speeding motorist, etc., who has been caught in the act of breaking the law, and/or justly arrested. Since around 1880. It is also used jocularly (since around 1920) as a general admission that one has been caught out, as in *'You're bluffing!' 'OK, it's a fair cop!'*

it's a free country an expression of tolerance, as in *I've no objection to* *nudist beaches – it's a free country.* Since the late 19th century. The phrase is also used defensively in response to a request, rule or law that places a restriction, however reasonable, on one's freedom, as in *'Would you mind not smoking in here, please.' 'It's a free country, isn't it?'; 'I'll park where I like – it's a free country, isn't it?'*

it's a great life if you don't weaken originally applied to life in the armed forces (since World War I); subsequently used in civilian life, with reference to a variety of activities and occupations. It is sometimes jocularly capped by the phrase 'but greater still if you do', i.e. if you yield to temptation (especially sexual temptation).

it's a hard life! used jocularly or ironically of a way of life that is anything but hard. Late 19th–20th centuries.

it's a living, already a mock-Jewish expression of resigned stoicism about one's job, as in *'Don't you ever get fed up with trying to persuade people to buy things they don't really want?' 'It's a living, already.'* Probably of US origin; adopted in the UK by 1960 at the latest. The phrase *it's a living* (or *it's a job*) may also be applied to any job, however unpleasant or poorly paid, that is better than none.

it's a long time between drinks a phrase traditionally attributed to John Motley Morehead, Governor of North Carolina in the early 1840s, who used it to restore amity and calm in a discussion with James H. Hammond, Governor of South Carolina, when the latter grew heated. It had achieved catch-phrase status in the USA by the late 19th century, and is occasionally used in the UK.

it's a new one on me see **new one on me, it's** (or **that's**) **a**.

it's a nice place to visit but I wouldn't want to live there a subjective opinion of any appropriate place, such as London (in British usage), New York City (in US usage) or Canberra (in Australian usage). Since around 1955.

it's a piece of cake applied to anything that is very easy to do. Since around 1938. The phrase is also used in other tenses, as in *it'll be a piece of cake, it was a piece of cake.* See also **it's a breeze; it's a doddle**.

it's a small world what a coincidence!; exclaimed at an unexpected meeting between two compatriots far from their own country, or between two strangers who find they have some distant connection, such as a friend or acquaintance in common, the same college, etc. Since around 1880.

it's against my religion a jocular excuse, as in *it's against my religion to subscribe to raffles; it's against my religion to partake of alcohol before lunch, but since you're twisting my arm . . ..* Since the mid-20th century. It may also be used to parry an invitation to do something risky, in place of the related phrase *I'm a devout coward.*

it's all clever stuff, y'know a comment upon anything that is baffling and/or impressive. Since around 1950. The phrase is often shortened to *it's all clever stuff* or *all clever stuff*.

it's all coming out now said when an argument reaches the stage where people lose their inhibitions and begin to bring up things that have been rankling for years. The phrase is also a jocular response to a confession (or an anticipated confession) of secret feelings, sexual misdemeanours, etc., as in '*. . . so Mary and I took refuge in this mountain hut for the night . . .' 'Aha, it's all coming out now!'* A catch phrase of the 20th century.

it's all done with mirrors see **all done with mirrors**.

it's all go life is a constant round of activity, pleasant or otherwise, as in *there's an office party Friday evening, a darts match at the pub Saturday lunchtime, the kids' swimming gala in the afternoon, then off to Anne and Pete's for dinner – it's all go, I tell you!*

it's all good clean fun said in mitigation after making fun of somebody, or after having fun at another's expense; also loosely applied to any amusement, entertainment, etc., which may or may not be as innocuous as the phrase suggests. Since around 1955.

it's all good for trade (often preceded by *ah, well!*) a philosophical response to or summary of a situation that has ended badly, or that has a disappointing outcome. The phrase probably originated in commerce during the 1920s or, at the latest, the 1930s.

it's all happening a lot of things are going on; also said jocularly or sarcastically when more than one thing happens at a time, often in the most trivial of circumstances, sometimes to emphasize that very triviality. The phrase has been used in a variety of senses since 1939 or earlier.

it's all money said to one who apologizes for handing over a large number of small coins as payment or change. Since around 1945.

it's all over bar the shouting see **all over bar the shouting**.

it's all part of life's rich pattern (or **pageant** or **tapestry**) see **all part of life's rich pattern**.

it's all (or **just**) **part of the service** a catch phrase that possibly originated in an advertising slogan for Austin Reed. It dates from the 1930s.

it's all right for some! see **all right for some!**

it's all water under the bridge see **water under the bridge**, **it's** (or **that's**) **all**.

it's anyone's bet see **anyone's bet**.

it's being so cheerful as keeps me going a catch phrase of the character Mona Lott, the depressed and unlucky laundrywoman played by

Joan Harben in the UK radio series *ITMA* (first broadcast in 1939).

it's curtains for you (or **him**, etc.)! see **curtains for you** (or **him**, etc.)!

it's good clean dirt a domestic catch phrase used when a morsel of food is dropped on the floor, but picked up and eaten. 20th century. The phrase is sometimes shortened to *it's clean dirt.*

it's got bells on that is a very old story or joke. Probably since around 1900 or earlier. The phrase may allude to the bells of a medieval court jester, who would have told such stories, or to the bell of a town crier. The variant *it's* (or *that's*) *got whiskers on it* dates back at least to the late 19th century. See also **pull the other one** (or **leg**) – **it's got bells on it!**; **with bells on**.

it's (just) one of those days uttered in a resigned or mock-despairing tone on one of those days when nothing appears to go right and much does go wrong. Probably since the 1920s. The phrase is also used in other tenses, as in *it's been one of those days*; John Wainwright's thriller *Cause for a Killing* (1974) begins: 'It was (as the saying goes) one of those days.' Similar sentiments are expressed in the phrase *it's (just) not my day.*

it's just one of those things applied to something inexplicable or inevitable. Since the mid-1930s, popularized by a Cole Porter song of the same name. The phrase is also used in other tenses, as in Nevil Shute's novel *The Chequer Board* (1947): 'It wasn't his fault he got taken by the Japs. It was just one of those things.'

it's like money in the bank said of a business or financial scheme that is certain to succeed, i.e. its expected proceeds are almost as real (if not quite as negotiable) as funds actually on deposit. A catch phrase of the 20th century.

it's like shooting fish in a barrel means 'it's dead easy', often with the implication that it is so easy as to be unfair or not worth doing. A simile that probably originated in the USA at the beginning of the 20th century or earlier.

it's made my day see **made my day, you've** (or **that's** or **it's**).

it's money for old rope refers to money that is very easily earned, or money that is paid for nothing or almost nothing. Since around 1905. A similar phrase is *it's money for jam*, which dates from around 1900.

it's naughty but it's nice see **little of what you fancy does you good, a**.

it's no go it's no use; it's impracticable or impossible. Since around 1820. The phrase was enshrined in English literature in the 1930s by Louis MacNeice's poem *Bagpipe Music*, with its constant refrain: 'It's no go the picture palace, it's no go the stadium, / . . . / It's no go the Government grants, it's no go the elections, / . . ..'

it's no skin off my nose it doesn't affect me adversely; an expression of indifference, as in *it's no skin off my nose if you drink yourself into an early grave*. Since around 1925 at the latest. The phrase probably originated in boxing or a similar activity. Variants (chiefly used by US males) substitute *ass* or *balls* for *nose*.

it's not cricket! see **not cricket!, it's** (or **that's**).

it's not done it's bad form; said of behaviour that is unacceptable in good society. Since the 1880s. The phrase is sometimes extended to *it's not done in the best of circles.*

it's not much if you say it quickly applied to a large sum of money, or a very high price or charge. The phrase has been in use since around 1910 or earlier.

it's not on it's unacceptable or intolerable; it's impractical or impossible. Since around 1960. Intensified variants include *it's just not on* and *it's simply not on*, as in *they expect us to work longer hours for less money – it's just not on!*

it's not the end of the world a consolatory expression; said to or by somebody who has suffered some mishap or disappointment, especially one that is not irremediable or irreversible. The phrase dates from around 1945.

it's not what you know but who you know influence is more important than ability; a cynical or bitter reference to the 'old-boy network' or something similar. Used in the US since around 1930 or earlier and in the UK from around 1945.

it's only money! a carefree, rueful or ironic attitude to expense or expenditure, as in *it cost me a hundred quid, but what the hell? It's only money!* The phrase dates from around 1925.

it's the gipsy (or **gypsy**) **in me** applied to impetuous behaviour, such as an impulse to have a wild, reckless love affair; also applied to an insatiable desire to travel or to be constantly on the move. A 20th-century catch phrase of US origin.

it's the (or **an**) **old army game** refers to 'the system', or to an attempt to beat or dodge the system. The phrase may also be applied to any abuse of trust, from a minor deception to a major swindle, or any instance of unfairness, favouritism, manipulation, exploitation, etc. It occurs in Theodore Fredenburgh's *Soldiers March* (1930): 'I get the idea. It's the old army game: first, pass the buck; second, ...' Of US origin; since the late 19th or early 20th century. The phrase *the old army game* originally referred to a gambling game.

it's the only game in town there is no alternative to the course of action under discussion. Probably since 1900 or earlier. From an anecdote about a faro addict who is warned that the game he plans to sit in on is notoriously crooked: he ruefully replies, 'I know, but it's the only game in town.'

it's the pits   applied to anything that is regarded by the speaker as the ultimate in objectionableness. (The word *pits* is probably short for *armpits*.) The phrase originally referred to a place; it is now also used, for example, of a plan of action or (with a name or *he*, *she*, etc., in place of *it*) a person. It originated in the USA around 1976 and was adopted in the UK around 1980. The US tennis player John McEnroe made famous a variant of the phrase after a dispute with a Wimbledon umpire in 1981; his alleged words are variously recorded as 'You are the pits of the world!' and 'This must be the pits!'

it's the same difference!   see **same difference!**

it's the thought that counts   a conventional or satirical cliché applied to a gift of very little value. It is sometimes uttered apologetically by the giver of such a gift, sometimes spitefully by the recipient.

it's time I wasn't here   see **time I wasn't here**.

it's your funeral   see **your funeral, it's** (or **that's**).

J

Jamaica see **Abyssinia!**

jobs for the boys refers to nepotism. Originally used in political contexts, the phrase was current in the 1930s but may have arisen much earlier.

join the club! sympathetically (or unsympathetically) addressed to one who has had an unpleasant experience or is in an undesirable situation that is shared by others, notably the speaker, as in *'I'm not getting a pay rise this year.' 'Join the club!'* The phrase has been in use in the UK and the USA since the late 1940s.

joint is jumping, the the place (e.g. a building or hall) is very lively. Used by enthusiasts of jazz, swing or pop music, especially in the USA, since the late 1930s.

jolly hockey sticks! a mildly derisive catch phrase referring to the jolly, hearty, games-loving atmosphere formerly associated with girls' public schools. It originated in the radio series *Educating Archie* (first broadcast in 1950), as the catch phrase of Archie's posh schoolgirl friend Monica, played by Beryl Reid. The phrase is sometimes used attributively.

just because you're paranoid, it doesn't mean to say they aren't all out to get you a retort to accusations that the speaker is paranoid (in the colloquial sense of 'obsessed by imaginary fears, suspicions, threats, dangers, etc.'). From the phrase *even paranoids have real enemies*, used in the USA from the late 1960s.

just fancy! an exclamation of astonishment or admiration, often used ironically. The phrase dates from around 1880 or earlier. It is an elaboration of the exclamation *fancy (that)!*

just for the hell of it see **for the hell of it**.

just for the record let me make my position clear; let's get things straight, as in *just for the record, I have no financial interest in any of the companies concerned*. Since around 1955. The phrase may have evolved from the idiomatic expression *to keep the record straight*.

just goes to show, it see **it just goes to show**.

just good friends see **we're just good friends**.

just part of the service see **it's all** (or **just**) **part of the service**.

just the job! this (or that) is exactly what I need. Used by the armed forces since around 1935, the phrase had entered general civilian usage by 1950.

just what the doctor ordered an expression of unqualified approval, applied to anything that is particularly welcome or apposite, or to anything exceptionally good or unexpectedly agreeable. A catch phrase of the 20th century.

K

keep on truckin'! keep on doing what you're doing; a general expression of encouragement. Since the 1930s. The phrase originated in the USA, where it was used in connection with the great marathon dance contests of the 1930s or with a type of lively dancing known as *truckin'* (from a song of the same name, written in the mid-1930s). There is also an obvious link with truck-driving, and the phrase came back into vogue on bumper stickers, etc., in the 1970s.

keep taking the tablets! a catch phrase that may have originated in radio or television comedy, perhaps *The Goon Show* (UK) or Morecambe and Wise. It has been in general use since the 1960s. In the late 1970s an advertisement for Pilsener lager featured the allusive slogan: 'Keep on taking the Pils!'

keep it under your hat! it's strictly confidential. A catch phrase of the late 19th–20th centuries. It may have been popularized by its repeated use in a song recorded by Jack Hulbert and Cicely Courtneidge in the mid-1920s: 'Keep it under your hat! / You must agree to do that. / Promise not to breathe a word, / In case it should be overheard.' The phrase was also used as a security slogan of World War II.

keep the faith(, baby) remain hopeful and steadfast; a valedictory catch phrase used between friends, especially in the USA in the 1960s. The phrase may have originated in Black or evangelical usage (or both).

keep your fingers crossed! wish me luck!; pray for me!; let's hope that this thing will happen or that this venture will prove successful, as in *I'm going to try again – keep your fingers crossed!* From around 1920. The phrase also occurs in the form *I'll keep my fingers crossed*, meaning 'I wish you luck', 'I hope it will happen', etc. The practice of crossing one's fingers for luck is probably related to the use of the sign of the Cross to ward off bad luck.

keep your hair on! don't lose your temper!; don't get over-excited! The phrase has been in use since around 1867.

keep your hand on your ha'penny a piece of advice to an unmarried girl (from the use of the word *ha'penny* as a slang term for the female genitals); the full form is . . . *till the right man turns up*. The phrase dates from around 1880 in this usage; during the 20th century it acquired the secondary meaning 'be careful or you'll find yourself expensively involved'. Both senses are now obsolescent. A variant of the phrase has *threepenny bit* in place of *ha'penny*.

keep your legs together! jocular advice to a girl or young woman to avoid sexual temptation or seduction; also used in the general sense of 'don't get screwed', literally or figuratively (i.e. swindled). A catch phrase of the 20th century, chiefly used in Australia and the USA. An international evangelist of the late 19th century used to say to his audience: 'Ladies, cross your legs! Gentlemen, the gates of hell are now closed.'

keep your pecker up! don't lose courage!; an exhortation to remain cheerful, optimistic, hopeful, resolute, etc. Since around 1840. From the use of the word *pecker* in the sense of 'courage' or 'resolution'; its use as a slang term for the penis, especially in the USA, is a potential cause of misunderstanding or *double entendre*.

keeping up with the Joneses keeping up with one's neighbours and friends in terms of material possessions and status symbols, usually prompted by a fear of appearing less well-off, important, smart, up-to-date, etc. The phrase was used as the title of a US comic strip as early as 1913; it came into vogue in the UK after World War II and achieved catch-phrase status on the marriage of Princess Margaret to Anthony Armstrong-Jones in 1960.

kill another canary and give the cat a treat! see **give the cat another goldfish!**

Kilroy was here a graffito. It was first used by US troops during World War II to mean 'the US army, or a US soldier, was here' and soon caught on in the UK; by 1942 the phrase had begun to appear on walls, etc., wherever British or US troops were stationed or fighting. The true identity of Kilroy is uncertain: a possible candidate is James J. Kilroy, a US politician and shipyard inspector who is said to have chalked the words 'Kilroy was here' on ships and crates that he had inspected.

kindly leave the stage see **I say, I say, I say!**

kiss me, Hardy! a jocular catch phrase of the late 19th–20th centuries; chiefly used in the armed forces. From Nelson's dying words to his flag-captain Thomas Masterman Hardy. (Certain historians believe that what Nelson actually said was 'Kismet, Hardy'.)

kiss my arse! an expression of utter incredulity or profound contempt; also used as an intensified negative. Since the mid-19th century or earlier. It is sometimes elaborated to *you* (or *he, she,* etc.)

can kiss my arse, as in the parody of the 'Red Flag' anthem: 'The working class can kiss my arse: I've got the foreman's job at last.' In US and Canadian usage *ass* is substituted for *arse.*

kiss of death, the refers to something that has disastrous or fatal consequences, as in *it'll be the kiss of death if she gets involved in the project.* Since the 1940s. The phrase is, of course, an allusion to the kiss from Judas Iscariot that betrayed Jesus Christ.

knock! knock! the introduction to a 'knock! knock!' joke, as in *'Knock! knock!' 'Who's there?' 'Mayonnaise.' 'Mayonnaise who?' 'Mayonnaise have seen the glory of the coming of the Lord!'* This use of the phrase may date back to the 19th century and remains extremely popular, especially among children. The phrase is also used by one who enters a room without knocking (or immediately after knocking, without waiting for a response).

L

large as life and twice as natural(**, as**) a catch phrase that may have originated in T. C. Haliburton's *The Clockmaker* (1837): 'He marched up and down afore the street door like a peacock, as large as life and twice as natural.' The phrase was further popularized in the UK by Lewis Carroll's use of it in *Through the Looking-Glass* (1871).

large mouth: large cunt see **big conk: big cock**.

last of the big spenders, the ironically applied to one who spends very little; also used self-deprecatingly of oneself, as in 'Do you want any raffle tickets?' 'Yes, give me 20p worth – the last of the big spenders, that's me!' The phrase may have originated in the USA in the 1920s or early 1930s, around the time of the Great Depression; it has been in general use in the UK since around 1945.

late for (one's) own funeral addressed or applied to somebody who is habitually and irritatingly unpunctual, as in *you'd be late for your own funeral*, *he'd* (or *she'd*) *be late for his* (or *her*) *own funeral*. A catch phrase of the 20th century.

laugh all the way to the bank see **cry all the way to the bank**.

laugh? I thought I should have died describes one's reaction to something highly amusing. The phrase dates from around 1880. There are numerous variants, including *laugh? I nearly bought my own beer*, *laugh? I nearly fell off the wife* and *laugh? I thought my pants would never dry!* See also **talk about laugh!**

lead me to it! with great pleasure!; that will be very easy! A catch phrase of the 20th century. The phrase occurs in Dorothy L. Sayers' *The Nine Tailors* (1934): '"Can you ride a motor-bike?" "Lead me to it, guv'nor!"'

lead on, Macduff! lead the way!; let's go!; let's get started! Late 19th–20th centuries. The phrase is a misquotation of a line from Shakespeare's *Macbeth*: 'Lay on, Macduff; / And damn'd be him that first cries, "Hold, enough!"'

let it all hang out! relax!; be uninhibited! The phrase was first used in the USA (especially by Blacks) in the 1960s, and rapidly spread to Canada and the UK. It is sometimes used with sexual connotations, or with punning reference to male or female nudity, as in the caption to a picture of bare-breasted girls in *Playboy*, December 1970.

let me tell you!   an emphatic tag, as in *it's not as easy as it looks, let me tell you!* The phrase has probably been used in the this way since around 1700, but did not achieve catch-phrase status until the 1930s or 1940s.

let the dog see the rabbit!   get out of the way (of somebody who wishes or needs to see or do something), as in *here's the electrician, he'll fix it – let the dog see the rabbit!* The phrase may have originated in the world of dog-racing, where it was in common use around 1938–50.

let's get the show on the road!   let's get moving!; let's get started! The phrase originated in the USA, perhaps as early as 1910, and has been used in the UK since around 1940. From the world of show business, especially touring companies. A minor variant has *this show* in place of *the show*.

let's have some light on the subject!   turn on the light(s)! A catch phrase of the 20th century. It is an example of an unusual sense development, from the figurative to the literal instead of the other way about.

let's not play games!   see **don't let's play games!**

let's run it up the flagpole (and see who salutes)   let's try it out and see what people's reactions are. Used in the USA since around 1950; also used in the UK.

let's try it on the dog!   see **try it on the dog!**

lie back and enjoy it!   applied to any unpleasant but presumably inescapable prospect or situation. The phrase was originally, and allegedly, used as advice to a girl or young woman when rape was inevitable. Since around 1950. See also **close your eyes and think of England!**

lies, damned lies and statistics   indicates an ascending order of mendacity. In Mark Twain's *Autobiography* (1924) the phrase is attributed to Benjamin Disraeli: 'There are three kinds of lies: lies, damned lies and statistics.' The phrase began its contemporary vogue after World War II.

life begins at forty   a catch phrase that originated as the title of a book by W. B. Pitkin (a US professor of journalism), published in 1932. It was further popularized as the title of a song by Jack Yellen and Ted Shapiro, recorded by Sophie Tucker in 1937. The phrase had become so embedded in the language by the mid-1950s that the number 40 in the game of bingo could be called simply 'life begins' (as an alternative to 'blind forty').

life is just a bowl of cherries   a catch phrase that originated in the US as the title of a song by Lew Brown and Ray Henderson, sung by

Ethel Merman in 1931. In the late 1970s Irma Bombeck used the phrase in the title of a book, *If Life Is a Bowl of Cherries, What Am I Doing in the Pits?*, a pun on *pits* in the sense of 'stones (of cherries, plums, etc.)' and in its slang usage (see **it's the pits**).

life is just one damned thing after another a comment upon life that has been variously attributed to the US writers Elbert Hubbard and Frank Ward O'Malley. The phrase was sufficiently well-known in the 1920s for the British writer John Masefield to use the initials of the last five words as the title of his novel *Odtaa* (1926).

life's too short a reason or excuse for not doing something, especially something that the speaker considers to be not worth the effort. The phrase occurs in a famous line from Henry James Byron's play *Our Boys*: 'Life's too short for chess.'

light the blue touchpaper and retire immediately! said when doing something risky. A traditional safety instruction for fireworks, the phrase was popularized by Arthur Askey in the UK radio series *Band Waggon* (first broadcast in 1938). The phrase appeared in the popular novel *Cider with Rosie*, Laurie Lee (1959): 'Dorothy, the next one, was a wispy imp, pretty and perilous as a firework. . . . her quick dark body seemed writ with warnings that her admirers did well to observe. "Not to be held in the hand," it said. "Light the touch-paper, but retire immediately."' The words *retire immediately* are sometimes replaced by *stand well clear*.

like a fart in a colander applied to somebody who is rushing around (especially anxiously and/or ineffectually) or running in and out, as in *he was tearing around like a fart in a colander, you're in and out like a fart in a colander – either stay in or get out!* 20th century. See also **rushing around like a blue-arsed fly**.

like a spare prick at a wedding unwanted, useless or idle, especially with a hint of embarrassed superfluity, as in *standing around like a spare prick at a wedding*. Since around 1880.

like hell I will! I certainly will not!; an emphatic refusal. Of US origin, the phrase dates from the mid-1940s. The word *hell* is sometimes replaced with something stronger.

like something the cat's brought in applied to one who looks utterly bedraggled or very disreputable, as in *go and tidy yourself up – you look like something the cat's brought in*. Since around 1920. See also **look what the cat's dragged in!**

like sparrows (or **geese**) **flying out of one's backside** a picturesque Australian catch phrase describing the male orgasm. Since around 1950 or earlier.

like the curate's egg see **good in parts, like the curate's egg**.

like there was no tomorrow refers to excess and recklessness of action, as in *spending money like there was no tomorrow*. Adopted from the USA in the 1970s. See also **spending money as if it were going out of fashion**.

little of what you fancy does you good, a a catch phrase that originated in the title of a song by Fred W. Leigh and George Arthurs, popularized by Marie Lloyd around 1900. It may refer to sex, alcohol, or any other 'forbidden fruit'. A similar phrase is *it's naughty but it's nice*, which is also derived from a popular song, of the same era.

little things please little minds refers to somebody who is doing something childish. There are a number of stock responses, including *while bigger fools* (or *smaller minds*) *look on, and little trousers fit little behinds, and large things have large behinds*, etc. The phrase has variant forms dating back to the 16th century or earlier, and the same idea was expressed by Ovid.

living on the smell of an oil-rag in a condition of extreme poverty. A chiefly Australian catch phrase that dates from the early 20th century.

living the life of Riley (or **Reilly**) having a carefree and comfortable life. An Anglo-Irish catch phrase of the 20th century.

long nose is a lady's liking, a see **big conk: big cock**.

long time no see! I haven't seen you for ages. The phrase derives from Chinese pidgin; it was introduced into the UK in the early 20th century via the Merchant Navy and the Royal Navy, and into the USA in the late 19th century by Chinese immigrants.

look, no hands! applied to something that is cleverly done. Since around 1910; from the proud claim of a child riding a bicycle with no hands on the handlebars. The phrase was used as the title of a comedy by Lesley Storm, which opened in London in 1971; it also occurs in a number of sick jokes, as in a caption to a picture of the Venus de Milo.

look what the cat's dragged in! see who's arrived! A jocular catch phrase of the 20th century. A variant is *look what the wind's blown in!* See also **like something the cat's brought in**.

look who's talking! addressed derisively to one who has no right to speak so censoriously, being equally guilty of whatever is under discussion, as in *'You drink too much.' 'Look who's talking!'* A catch phrase of the 20th century. A variant is *you can talk!*

look you! applied or addressed to a Welsh person by another British national, alluding or responding to a decidedly Welsh characteristic. Late 19th–20th centuries. The phrase is a well-known Cymricism dating back to the 16th century or earlier: in Shakespeare's *Henry V* the Welshman Fluellen uses it very frequently – eleven times in the scene in which he first appears.

looks like a million dollars, he (or **she**)   he (or she) looks extremely attractive; often applied to somebody wearing expensive (or expensive-looking) clothing, as in *she looks like a million dollars in that coat*. Since around 1920 at the latest. The phrase also occurs in the form *you look like a million dollars*, addressed to such a person. The related idiom *to feel like a million dollars* means 'to feel very happy, well, proud, etc.'.

looks like a wet weekend(**, it**)   used by girls or women menstruating at the weekend; also addressed by a male to a female carrying what looks like a packet of tampons or sanitary towels. Chiefly used in Australia, since around 1930 (for the first sense) or 1940 (for the second sense). In the UK the phrase *he* (or *she*) *looks like a wet weekend* is applied to a particularly gloomy-looking person.

love you and leave you, I must (or **I'll**)   see **I must love you and leave you**.

lovely weather for ducks!   see **fine weather for ducks!**

low man on a (or **the**) **totem pole**(**, the**)   the lowest-ranking, least successful, etc., individual in a group or organization. The phrase was used as a the title of a book by H. Allen Smith (1941, published in the UK in 1947). A 'Peanuts' strip-cartoon of 1982, by Charles Schulz, featured the following exchange between Linus and Lucy: "'I was hoping to lie in the beanbag, and watch TV . . ..' "Too bad," says Lucy, "I got here first." "That's the story of my life . . .. Low man on the beanbag!"'

lower than a snake's belly   applied to an utterly contemptible and despicable person or act. Chiefly Australian; also used in the UK and the USA since around 1945. Variants of the phrase have *hips* or *elbows* in place of *belly*.

lucky as a bastard on Father's Day(**, as**)   see **happy as a bastard on Father's Day**.

lucky one!, aren't you (or **I**) **the**   a congratulatory catch phrase that is sometimes sincere, but usually sarcastic or ironic. Since the 1920s. The phrase is also used in other persons, as in *'She's won a weekend at a health farm.' 'Isn't she the lucky one!'*

M

made my day, you've (or **that's** or **it's**)   applied to a remark (whether flattering or sincere) or incident (from the trivial to the momentous) that has made me happy, restored my confidence, etc. Since the late 1940s. In modern usage the phrase is sometimes an ironic comment upon something unexpected and unwelcome.

make love, not war!   a pacifist slogan that is used allusively, jocularly or derisively as a catch phrase. Of US origin, the slogan was adopted in the UK by hippies, flower people, etc., in the mid-1960s and had developed into a catch phrase by the end of the decade.

make no mistake!   used for emphasis, as in *she's a highly respected member of the profession, make no mistake!* The phrase may have originated in the USA around 1850. In British usage the extended form *make no mistake about it* is perhaps more frequent, as in *make no mistake about it, the country is on the road to ruin!* See also **and no mistake**.

makes you think, doesn't it?   a response to (or comment upon) something surprising, remarkable, suspicious, etc. The phrase may have originated in Cockney usage (in the form *makes yer think, don't it?*) in the 1870s or 1880s. In modern usage *don't* is often jocularly substituted for *doesn't.*

man's gotta do what a man's gotta do, a   applied jocularly to any act or duty, however trivial, guying the literal usage of the phrase as a piece of homespun philosophy (the sort of thing that the US actor John Wayne might have said in one of his 'he-man' film roles, though its actual origin is uncertain). Adopted from the USA around 1945 or earlier. See also **when you gotta go, you gotta go!**

many thanks for those few kind words   see **thank you for those few kind words**.

maybe they know something we don't   we're doing this – I wonder why they're doing that? Perhaps they have inside information denied to us, as in *they've gone the long way round – maybe they know something we don't.* The phrase may also be used ironically or jocularly, and/or with *he knows* or *she knows* in place of *they know*. Since the 1960s or earlier.

me and my big mouth!   I shouldn't have said that!; an exclamation or apology made when one reveals a secret, opens one's mouth and puts one's foot in it, etc. The phrase has been in general use in the USA since around 1940 and is also common in the UK.

me Tarzan, you Jane you are a woman, I am a man. The phrase is popularly associated with film versions of Edgar Rice Burroughs' *Tarzan* stories, though it does not occur in the latter and has not been traced to any specific film. The US actor Johnny Weissmuller, who played the title role in *Tarzan the Ape Man* (1932) and subsequent films, is quoted in *Photoplay* magazine (June 1932) as saying 'I didn't have to act in *Tarzan the Ape Man* – just said, "Me Tarzan, you Jane."' However, what he actually said in the film was just 'Tarzan . . . Jane'.

meanwhile, back at the ranch used to recall one's listeners to the main theme of one's narrative, to bring a conversation back to its central point, or in any similar situation; sometimes no more than an elaboration of the word *meanwhile*. (The word *ranch* is occasionally replaced with another word, used either because it is more appropriate or for jocular effect.) The phrase has been used in the USA since the 1920s and is equally well known in the UK. Its origin lies in the old silent Westerns, where a stirring fight between cowboys and Indians was often interrupted by this caption, introducing a flashback to the ranch.

meeting like this, we can't go on (or **we must stop**) said by either of two people coincidentally meeting again within a short time and/or in some inappropriate place (e.g. a crowded lift, a public convenience, etc.). A catch phrase of the later 20th century. It may have originated as a line from some melodramatic play or film, uttered by star-crossed lovers meeting in secret.

men are only interested in one thing i.e. sexual intercourse; a cynical catch phrase used by women that probably dates from around 1880 or earlier. It is sometimes applied or addressed to an individual, with *he is* or *you're* in place of *men are*. Another variant of the phrase occurs in an article by Martyn Harris in *New Society* (1 March 1984): 'A man tried to steal the money she [a prostitute] carries in a concealed pocket in her skirt. . ... "Men are only after one thing," she says, and I don't like to ask whether it's money or sex that she means.'

merry Christmas to you too! see **and a merry Christmas to you too!**

message received I understand what you're getting at; I get the point – there's no need to go on and on about it! Since the mid-1940s. From the literal use of the phrase in signalling, telecommunications, etc., especially by the armed forces during World War II.

miaow! miaow! said by or to somebody who makes a malicious or spiteful remark about another, or who is engaged in gossip of this nature. Since the early 1920s. The phrase is probably an allusion to the use of the adjective *catty* in the sense of 'spiteful; malicious'.

mighty white of you!, that's see **that's mighty** (or **damn**) **white of you!**

miles and miles and bloody miles of sweet fuck-all a ruefully jocular description of the African desert, the Canadian prairies, or any similar expanse of flat, desolate land. The phrase was first used (with reference to the African desert) during World War I. A more polite variant substitutes *bugger all* for *sweet fuck-all*.

mind boggles, the a comment upon any marked absurdity, or upon anything that is difficult to comprehend or imagine, as in *I wonder what he was trying to do when he got his finger stuck – the mind boggles!* Since the 1950s or earlier. The phrase may have been popularized by the strip-cartoon 'The Perishers', by Maurice Dodd and Dennis Collins, which first appeared in the *Daily Mirror* in the late 1950s.

mind how you go! look after yourself; take care; be careful; addressed, for example, to somebody departing, stumbling, embarking on a risky enterprise, etc. The phrase has been in common use since around 1942.

mind you, I've said nothing perhaps I shouldn't have said that, so don't quote me. An Anglo-Irish catch phrase of the 20th century.

mind your backs! excuse me, I wish to get past (or through); get out of the way!; said jocularly by one encumbered with an unwieldy load, pushing a trolley or wheelbarrow, etc. Since the early 20th century. From the use of the phrase by railway porters moving goods or luggage.

mission accomplished the job has been done; the purpose has been fulfilled. Originally a military formula, the phrase has been used in the USA since 1942 and, less frequently, in the UK from 1944.

mixture as before, the the same (drink) again; a reply to the question 'What'll you have?' The phrase is also applied to any rehash of the same old ingredients, features, ideas, etc., e.g. in an electoral campaign. Since around 1920. Probably from the literal use of the phrase by those prescribing or dispensing pharmaceutical preparations, such as cough mixture.

money talks refers to the power or influence of money, the advantages or privileges conferred by wealth, etc.; a semi-proverbial catch phrase.

monkey see, monkey do! applied e.g. to a task that is learnt and subsequently performed with reasonable competence, but never actually understood, as in *I know which keys to press, but it's monkey see, monkey do – I haven't a clue why I'm doing it, or what's going on inside the* *computer!* The phrase may also be addressed to anybody who imitates the actions of another, or used as a warning against doing something that might be copied by another (especially a child). Used in the USA and Canada around 1925 and in the UK from around 1950.

more fun than a barrel of monkeys   tremendous fun, as in *have a go – it's more fun than a barrel of monkeys!* The phrase was probably in common use before 1920.

more power to your elbow!   good for you!; An expression of encouragement used to indicate that something would be an impressive achievement, as in *Well if you can get that to work, more power to your elbow.* Possibly since the mid-19th century; of Anglo-Irish origin.

more than somewhat   means 'very much'. The phrase was popularized by the US writer Damon Runyon, who used it frequently and effectively in his newspaper columns of the 1920s and 1930s, in the work that made him internationally famous, *Guys and Dolls* (1932), and as the title of a book published in 1937.

more than you could poke (or **shake**) **a stick at**   a very great quantity of the thing in question (usually money), as in *she's got more money than you could poke* (or *shake*) *a stick at.* The phrase dates from the 19th century.

morning after the night before, the   refers to a hangover, the delayed after-effects of a drinking-bout. A catch phrase of the 20th century.

mox nix   it makes no difference; it doesn't matter. A corruption of the German phrase *es macht nichts,* used by US and British troops stationed in Germany after World War II and by civilians from around 1950.

must you stay? can't you go?   jocularly addressed to those who have overstayed their welcome. The phrase may have been popularized in this form by a *Punch* cartoon of 1905, but it probably originated in the 19th century in the form *must you go? can't you stay?,* used by the schoolmaster Charles John Vaughan to speed up the departure of boys invited to breakfast and too shy to take their leave.

mustn't grumble   see **fair to middling**.

mutton dressed as lamb   applied to a middle-aged or elderly person (especially a woman) dressed in an unbecomingly youthful fashion. Since the late 19th century.

my arse is dragging   I am so exhausted that I can hardly walk. The phrase probably dates from around 1910. US variants have *ass, butt* or *tail* in place of *arse;* another (masculine) variant is *my balls are hanging low.*

my belly thinks my throat's cut   see **my stomach thinks my throat's cut**.

my (or **her**) **country cousins have come**   see **captain is at home, the**.

my dogs are barking my feet are sore. Adopted from US servicemen towards the end of World War II. From the slang use of *dogs* in the sense of 'feet'. See also **my feet are killing me**.

my elbow! see **my foot!**

my feet are killing me my feet are very sore (especially as a result of too much standing or walking). Used chiefly by women, the phrase dates from around 1890. See also **my dogs are barking**.

my foot! an exclamation of emphatic disbelief, as in *'It was an accident.' 'Accident, my foot!'* Other parts of the body, such as *eye* or *arse*, may be substituted for *foot*; a chiefly US variant is *my elbow!*

my guts are beginning to think my throat's cut see **my stomach thinks my throat's cut**.

my heart bleeds for you said with heavy or bitter irony, expressing a lack of sympathy, as in *'If I don't find a job soon, I may have to sell the yacht.' 'My heart bleeds for you.'* Other personal pronouns may be substituted for *you*. Since the late 1940s. The phrase *you're breaking my heart*, also heavily ironic, is used in similar circumstances.

my hero! a jocular or ironic response to male bravado; also addressed or applied to one who does something that actually requires little courage or involves no danger. Since the 1950s or earlier.

my lips are sealed a refusal to pass comment, answer a question, divulge a secret, etc. The phrase is traditionally associated with the British prime minister Stanley Baldwin, who is alleged to have used it on a number of occasions. What he actually said, in a speech on 10 December 1935, was: 'My lips are not yet unsealed.'

my spies are everywhere see **I have my agents**.

my stomach thinks my throat's cut I'm very hungry. A catch phrase that dates back to the 16th century. Variants include *my belly thinks my throat's cut* and *my guts are beginning to think my throat's cut*, which date from the 18th century.

my wife doesn't understand me the traditional complaint made by a man seeking sympathy and, sooner or later, sexual satisfaction outside marriage. Probably since time immemorial. The phrase is occasionally used by women, with *husband* in place of *wife*.

N

name of the game, the refers to the crux of the matter, the predominant factor, true purpose, real nature, etc., as in *the name of the game is survival; sexploitation is the name of the game*. Used in the USA since the early 1960s and in the UK from around 1965. See also **that's the name of the game**.

name your poison! what would you like to drink? The phrase probably originated in the USA in the late 19th century, perhaps reflecting the temperance movement slogan 'Alcohol is poison'; it has been used in the UK since the 1920s.

natives are restless tonight, the refers to a restless, unruly or hostile audience, especially in the theatre (but also at political gatherings, etc.). The phrase also occurs in the form *the natives are getting restless*, jocularly referring to hostile residents, dissatisfied customers, impatient guests, unruly children, etc. It probably dates from the days of British rule in India or the African colonies.

naughty, naughty! an admonition used jocularly among adults. Since around 1950.

need I say more? see **nudge, nudge, wink, wink!**

never a dull moment! said at times of great excitement, danger or stress, or ironically on less exciting, dangerous or stressful occasions. The phrase has been in general use since around 1945.

never darken my door (or **doorstep**) **again!** go away and don't come back!, as in *get out, and never darken my door again!* The phrase originated in 19th-century melodrama, addressed, for example, to an dishonoured daughter or dishonourable son; in modern usage it is chiefly jocular.

never explain and never apologize a 20th-century maxim that is attributed to the British admiral John Arbuthnot 'Jacky' Fisher, who wrote in a letter to *The Times*, 5 September 1919: 'Never contradict. Never explain. Never apologize. (Those are the secrets of a happy life!)' The similar phrase *never complain and never explain* has been attributed to both Benjamin Disraeli and Stanley Baldwin.

never fear: . . . is here (with the speaker's name in place of the ellipsis) an expression of jocular reassurance, with the implication that the speaker will provide protection, put right whatever has gone wrong, etc. Possibly since around 1920.

never give a sucker an even break! a catch phrase of the US comedian W. C. Fields, who popularized it in the 1920s and subsequently used it as the title of a film (1941), the plot of which he allegedly wrote on the back of an envelope and sold for $25,000. It is not known whether Fields actually coined the phrase, which has also been attributed to others.

never had it so good, you've (or **they've**, etc.) you (or they, etc.) have no cause for complaint, being better off now than ever before. In the UK the phrase is traditionally associated with the Conservative prime minister Harold Macmillan, who said in a speech on 20 July 1957: 'Let us be frank about it: most of our people have never had it so good.' It had been used in the USA, however, since the mid-1940s or earlier, in the form *you* (or *they*, etc.) *never had it so good*, and may be of German origin.

never mind the quality: feel the width! used since the mid-20th century in ironic parody of sales patter or spiel; applied more seriously in the later 20th century to the necessity of eking out meagre resources (e.g. government aid) to cover an impossibly large and neglected field. The phrase was popularized as the title of a UK television comedy series, set in an East End tailoring business, in the late 1960s.

never say die! an expression of encouragement; also used jocularly or ironically as a catch phrase since around 1915.

never shit where you eat see **don't shit on your own doorstep**.

new one on me, it's (or **that's**) **a** this is the first time I've heard of (or seen) that, as in *my daughter says everybody's doing it these days, but it's a new one on me*. The phrase dates from around 1920.

nice bit o' cloth you got there, my boy addressed to somebody wearing a new suit, jacket or coat. (The phrase is usually uttered in a mock-Jewish accent and accompanied by the act of rubbing the new lapel between the speaker's thumb and fingers.) Probably of music-hall origin.

nice guys finish last a catch phrase attributed to Leo Durocher, manager of the Brooklyn Dodgers baseball team. A book of the same name, published in 1975, contains the following statement made by Durocher on 6 July 1946: 'I called off his players' names as they came marching up the steps behind him, "Walker, Cooper, . . . Thomson. Take a look at them. All nice guys. They'll finish last. Nice guys. Finish last."' The phrase rapidly caught on in the USA, at first among baseball fans, and is also used in the UK.

nice (little) place you've got here applied ironically to a very grand residence or, less frequently, to a hovel. The phrase was popularized in the 1940s by Tommy Handley, star of the radio series *ITMA*, who made this remark when the programme was performed at Windsor Castle on 21 April 1942.

nice place to live out of, (it's) a see **good place to be from, (it's) a**.

nice weather for ducks! see **fine weather for ducks!**

nice work if you can get it applied to a very favourable or agreeable arrangement or situation, such as a job with attractive fringe benefits. The phrase was used as the title of a song (1937) by George and Ira Gershwin, with the following refrain: 'Nice work if you can get it, / And you can get it if you try.' It may an extension of the phrase *nice work!*, an exclamation of warm approval of something well done.

nil carborundum see **illegitimis non carborundum**.

no, but you hum it and I'll pick up the tune a facetious response to any question that begins 'Do you know . . .?', as in *'Do you know you've got a hole in your tights?' 'No, but you hum it and I'll pick up the tune.'* Late 19th–20th centuries. A modern variant has *I'll play it* in place of *I'll pick up the tune*. The phrase was originally addressed e.g. by a pub pianist to a member of the audience who asked 'Do you know [name of song or tune]?'

no can do I can't do it; that's impossible, as in *'Have you got change for a fiver?' 'No can do.'* Sometimes abbreviated to *NCD*. The phrase originated in pidgin English, probably around 1830. It is the negative form of **can do**, which it may predate by some 20 years.

no chance! an emphatic negative. The phrase has been in general use since the early 1970s, but has been superseded to some extent by **no way!**

no comment! I do not wish to pass comment on that issue, answer that question, etc.; used jocularly by the general public in imitation of politicians, show-business personalities and other famous people who give this evasive response to reporters, television interviewers, etc. (It has been suggested that the phrase often means 'What you say is true, but I am not (yet) prepared to admit it.') Since around 1950.

no dice! definitely not!; not a chance!; no luck!, as in *I tried to persuade her, but no dice!* Used in the USA and Canada since around 1925 or earlier; also used in the UK. The phrase is of gambling origin.

no flies on him (or **her**), **there are** he (or she) is nobody's fool. A variant is *no flies on me!* The phrase also occurs in the extended form *there are no flies on him* (or *her*) *– but you can see where they've been*, which probably dates back to the early 20th century.

no go, it's   see **it's no go**.

no harm in trying(**, there's**)   said jocularly by or to one who gives short change, absent-mindedly pockets something belonging to another, etc. The victim might add . . . *that's how I got it!* Since 1900 or earlier.

no, I'm with the Woolwich   see **are you with me?**

no joy   see **any joy?**

no kidding? (or !)   really?; You don't say! Used in the USA since the late 19th century and in the UK from around 1920. The phrase occurs in John Lange's novel *Binary* (1972): '"We're going to Phoenix," Peters said. "No kidding," the woman said. "That's my home town."

no names, no pack drill   said by one who does not wish to involve another or others by mentioning their names, as in *there's a man I know – no names, no pack drill – who can get you a false passport.* Used in the armed services since around 1890 and by civilians from around 1919. Pack drill was a military punishment that involved marching with a heavy pack.

no offence (meant) – none taken(, I'm sure)   a catch-phrase exchange that occurs in any appropriate situation; the reply is often uttered in a mock-genteel tone of voice. Probably since the early 20th century.

no prizes for guessing . . .   applied to something that is quite obvious, as in *no prizes for guessing where she spent the night; only one person failed: no prizes for guessing who that was!* Since the late 1940s.

no rest for the wicked!(**, there's**)   said by or to somebody who is kept extremely busy. A catch phrase of the 19th–20th centuries that originated in the Bible (Isaiah 48:22): 'There is no peace, saith the Lord, unto the wicked.'

no sir(ree)!   an emphatic negative, as in *I'm not a vindictive person, no sirree!* Used in the USA since the mid-19th century or earlier and in the UK from around 1920.

no skin off my nose, it's   see **it's no skin off my nose**.

no sweat!   it is (or was or will be) no trouble; don't worry, as in *sure, I can do that for you: no sweat!* Used in the USA since around 1935 or earlier; also used in the UK.

no way!   absolutely not!; an expression of emphatic negation, denial, refusal, etc. Adopted from the USA around 1974. The phrase is also used in the more specific sense of 'it's impossible', elliptical for 'there's no way it can be done' or something similar. See also **no chance!**

none the better for your asking   an abrupt rejection of conventional

solicitude, as in *'How are you?' 'None the better for your asking!'* Since
the late 17th century; chiefly jocular in modern usage. A variant
(since the late 18th century) is *no better for your asking.*

not a bad drop, this!   this is excellent liquor! A 20th-century catch
phrase of Australian origin.

not a cat in hell's chance   no chance whatsoever, as in *we haven't got a
cat in hell's chance of winning.* A 20th-century variant of the phrase *no
more chance than a cat in hell without claws,* which dates from around
1750, when it was chiefly applied to the underdog in a dispute or
quarrel. See also **as much chance as a snowball in hell**.

not a pretty sight   applied to any unattractive or ugly sight, scene, etc.,
as in *he came to the door in his underpants: not a pretty sight!* The phrase
was used by D. A. N. Jones in the *Listener,* 16 October 1980: 'But if
any gatecrasher gets in, they jump on him, hard, just like SAS men.
Not a pretty sight.' It was popularized by the British comedians Eric
Morecambe and Ernie Wise on the *Morecambe and Wise Show,* first
broadcast on television in the 1960s.

not all it's cracked up to be(, it's)   see **not what (or all) it's cracked up
to be(, it's)**.

not as (or so) green as I'm cabbage-looking, I'm   I'm not *that* stupid,
foolish, gullible, etc. Since the mid-19th century. Other personal
pronouns may be used in place of *I.*

not bloody likely!   an intensification of the phrase *not likely!* Late 19th–
20th centuries. The phrase was popularized by the Cockney character Eliza Doolittle in Shaw's play *Pygmalion* (1912): 'Walk! Not bloody
likely. I am going in a taxi.' This gave rise to the 'literary' variant *not
Pygmalion likely!* (An authority on Cockney usage has suggested that
in real life Eliza would probably have been more likely to say 'No
bleedin' fear!')

not cricket!, it's (or that's)   it's (or that's) unfair; it's (or that's) un-
sportsmanlike. An essentially British catch phrase that has always
puzzled Americans and other foreigners. Since the late 19th or early
20th century. The phrase occurs in Stanley Houghton's play *The
Partners* (1913): 'It may even enable you to take high place in the
ranks of the emancipated – but it is not playing the game. In other
words, Cynthia, it is not cricket.'

not half!   an exclamation of emphatic affirmation or agreement, as in
'Did you like it?' 'Not half!' The phrase originated in Cockney usage
around 1905.

not if I see you first!   see **see you!**

not in front of the children!   a warning against indiscretion, used jocularly or ironically as a catch phrase. Since the early 20th century.

The phrase has the variant *pas devant les enfants* (or *domestiques*), which relies on the assumption that the children (or servants) do not understand French.

not in the same ball-park   see **in the same ball-park**.

not much!   an expression of emphatic contradiction, used with heavy irony, as in *'I didn't mean to upset her.' 'Not much (you didn't)!'* (i.e. you certainly did!); *'Surely he wouldn't swindle his own brother.' 'Not much (he wouldn't)!'* (i.e. he certainly would!). The phrase has been used in this way since the 1930s or earlier.

not on your life!   certainly not! A catch phrase that dates from the 1880s or earlier. It occurs in Edward Albee's play *Who's Afraid of Virginia Woolf?* (1962): 'Look here, kid, you don't think for a second I'm going to let you publish this crap. Not on your life, baby.' There are a number of variants, notably **not on your nelly!**

not on your nelly (or **Nelly** or **Nellie**)**!**   a variant of **not on your life!** Since the late 1930s. *Nelly* is short for *Nelly* (or *Nellie*) *Duff*, rhyming slang for 'puff', referring to the breath of life.

not Pygmalion likely!   see **not bloody likely!**

not quite quite   not quite the thing; not acceptable in polite society, as in *her behaviour? Well, not quite quite, you know, he's not quite quite – a bit of a rough diamond.* The phrase dates from the late 19th century and enjoyed a revival in the 1920s; it is still used in upper-middle-class society. See also **too too**.

not so as (or **so's**) **you'd notice (it)**   not noticeably; not really, as in *'Has it made any difference?' 'Not so's you'd notice.'* Since the late 1920s.

not so green as I'm cabbage-looking, I'm   see **not as** (or **so**) **green as I'm cabbage-looking, I'm**.

not to worry!   don't worry; there's nothing to worry about; it doesn't matter, as in *not to worry! I've got a spare.* The phrase may have originated in the armed forces in the mid-1930s.

not tonight, Josephine   a jocular refusal or rejection of any request, offer, invitation, etc.; originally used in sexual contexts. Late 19th–20th centuries. The phrase is apocryphally attributed to Napoleon Bonaparte, with reference to the legendary sexual appetite of his wife Josephine de Beauharnais. It was popularized as the title of a song (1915) by Worton David and Lawrence Wright.

not waving but drowning   applied to an apparent indication of well-being that is actually a sign of distress. The phrase originated in a poem of the same name by Stevie Smith (1957): 'Nobody heard him, the dead man, / But still he lay moaning: / I was much further out than you thought / And not waving but drowning.'

not what (or all) it's cracked up to be(, it's)   it falls short of its reputation; often applied to sex. Since around 1910.

nothing for nothing, and very little for tuppence-ha'penny (**,** **you get**) a catch phrase that is said to have been coined by George Bernard Shaw around 1910. It is reminiscent of a *Punch* cartoon caption of 1869: 'Nothink for nothink 'ere, and precious little for sixpence.'

nothing to write home about   applied to something unremarkable, unimpressive, unexciting, etc., as in *it was pretty average – nothing to write home about.* The phrase dates from the late 19th century.

now **he tells me!**   see *now* **you tell me!**

now I've seen (or **heard**) **everything!**   an ironic expression of mock wonder; said in response to something highly unusual, unexpected, ridiculous, incredible, etc., as in *well, old Mr Robinson riding a motorbike – now I've seen everything!*; *'She says the cat ate it.' 'Now I've heard everything!'*

now tell me the one about the three bears   see **have you any more funny stories?**

now then, what's all this 'ere?   a variant of **hello, hello, hello!**

now you see it, now you don't   applied to anything that suddenly disappears (or seems to disappear), or to any instance of trickery, deception or cover-up. The phrase may also be applied to people, with *he, she,* etc., in place of *it.* Since around 1930. From conjurors' patter.

now **you tell me!**   said in response to information that comes too late to be of use, as in *'It's a good job her parents weren't there – her father's a policeman.' 'Now you tell me!'* The original form of the phrase, adopted from the USA in the 1950s, has *he* in place of *you,* as in *'You didn't need to break the door down – I've got a key.' 'Now he tells me!'*

now you're talking!   said in response to a suggestion, offer, etc., that the speaker approves of or finds (more) acceptable, as in *'Would you like a drink?' 'Now you're talking!'*; *'How about £500, with a 10% bonus if the work is finished on time?' 'Now you're talking!'* Since around 1880.

nudge, nudge, wink, wink!   a catch phrase associated with the television series *Monty Python's Flying Circus,* where it was used with sexual innuendo in a sketch first broadcast in 1969: 'Your wife . . . does she, er, does she "go" – eh? eh? eh? Know what I mean, know what I mean? Nudge nudge. Say no more.' (The words *wink, wink* occur later in the sketch.) In general usage it may be applied to any situation of doubtful morality, legality, etc. The phrase is often followed by *say no more!*, as in the *Monty Python* sketch, or by *need I say more?*

nuff said!   see **enough said!**

nutty as a fruitcake (**,** **as**)   crazy; extremely eccentric, as in *her father is as nutty as a fruitcake.* Used in the USA since around 1920 and in the UK from around 1945.

O

of all the nerve! a highly indignant response to barefaced effrontery, as in *they asked for their money back – of all the nerve!* Adopted from the USA around 1918. Variants include *what a nerve!, you've got a nerve!, I like your nerve!,* etc.

off like a bride's nightie applied to somebody or something that departs promptly or speedily, as in *he was off like a bride's nightie when he found out.* A chiefly Australian catch phrase that dates from around 1960. See also **up and down like a bride's nightie**.

oh, brother! an exclamation of dismay, horror, irritation, exasperation, etc. A US catch phrase of the 20th century that is also known in the UK, where it was used as the title of a television comedy series featuring Derek Nimmo as a member of a religious order.

oh, come on! an exhortation to show some intelligence, to react sensibly to the obvious, etc., as in *oh, come on! You don't expect me to believe that, do you?* Later 20th century.

oh, la! la! an exclamation of delighted astonishment, of French origin. Used in the UK since the early 20th century. The phrase also occurs in the form *oo-la-la!*, which may be used as a noun with sexual connotations, as in *a bit of oo-la-la.*

oh, mother, is it worth it? used jocularly or ironically, mostly by women, in any appropriate situation. 20th century. In 1960 Arnold Wesker published a pamphlet called *The Modern Playwright or 'Oh, Mother, is it worth it?'*, referring to his early uphill struggle to make a living with his plays. The phrase originally referred to the pain of childbirth.

oh, my giddy aunt! an exclamation of surprise, usually uttered with rueful humour. Since the early 20th century; perhaps inspired by Brandon Thomas's long-running farcical comedy *Charley's Aunt* (1892). A less frequent variant is *oh, my sainted aunt!*

oi, oi! used to interrupt or remonstrate with somebody who is holding forth or laying down the law; also used as an exclamation of incredulity or mock incredulity, as in *oi, oi! What's going on here?* In US Yiddish usage the phrase has a multitude of meanings.

okay by me! (, **it's** or **that's**) an expression of assent, agreement, acceptance, approval, etc. Adopted from the USA around 1932. The words *by me* suggest that the phrase is a loan translation from the Yiddish *bei mir*. The corresponding interrogative form is *okay by you?*

okey-doke!   okay! A reduplicated form that dates from the 1930s. It is often extended to okey-*dokey!*

old army game, it's the (or **an**)   see **it's the** (or **an**) **old army game**.

old as my tongue and a little older than my teeth(, **as**)   a smart or evasive reply to the question 'How old are you?' The phrase dates back to the late 17th century.

old enough to know better   usually used in an admonitory sense, as in *'You should be ashamed of yourself – you're old enough to know better'*. Since the mid-19th century. The phrase sometimes occurs in the extended form . . . *but young enough to do it anyway.*

old soldiers never die: they only fade away   from a 20th-century army parody of the song 'Kind Thoughts Can Never Die': 'Old soldiers never die – / They simply fade away. / . . . / Old soldiers never die – / Young ones wish they would.' The phrase may be jocularly adapted to fit a wide range of activities or occupations, as in *old golfers never die: they just lose their balls* and *old lexicographers never die: they simply lose their meaning.*

on a hiding to nothing   bound to fail; bound to be defeated, as in *the government is on a hiding to nothing*. Since around 1960.

on cloud nine   blissfully or ecstatically happy, as in *she was on cloud nine when she heard she'd got the job*. Adopted from the USA around 1972.

on my shit list, he's (or **you're**)   applied or addressed to somebody who has done something for which the speaker is determined to get even. Since around 1940 or earlier. The phrase *shit list* may be a pun on *short list* (for a job, promotion, etc.) or *hit list* (of a gangster, terrorist group, etc.)

on with the motley!   let's begin (a party, an expedition to the theatre, etc.)!; also used by one who must proceed despite difficulties, or in circumstances similar to those of *the show must go on* (see **show must go on, the**). The phrase comes from Ruggiero Leoncavallo's opera *I Pagliacci* (1892); it is a translation of '*Vesti la giubba*', the cry of the clown who must make others laugh while his own heart is breaking. (The word *motley* denotes the costume of a jester.)

on your (or **yer**) **bike!**   off you go!; go away! The phrase dates from around 1960. Since the 1980s it has been associated with the Conservative politician Norman Tebbit, who made the following remark while Secretary of State for Employment (1981): 'I grew up in the Thirties with our unemployed father. He did not riot, he got on his bike and looked for work.'

once aboard the lugger and the girl is mine   a derisively jocular catch phrase of the late 19th–20th centuries, favoured by men. It is based on the following quotation from John Benn Johnstone's *The Gipsy Farmer*: 'I want you to assist me in forcing her on board the lugger; once there, I'll frighten her into marriage.'

once is enough! applied to any appropriate experience, especially marriage (said, for example, by a divorced or widowed person). A catch phrase of the 20th century. It was popularized as the title of a witty comedy by Frederick Lonsdale, produced in 1938.

one for the book(, **that's**) refers to a joke so funny, an event so extraordinary or an achievement so remarkable that it merits inclusion in a book of jokes, extraordinary events, remarkable achievements, etc. The phrase has been used in this way in the USA since the 1940s and in the UK from around 1955. (It has also been used in the RAF, and possibly elsewhere, with reference to a gross exaggeration; this sense dates from the early 1920s.)

one for the road the last of several drinks, especially a final drink offered to or consumed by one who is about to leave for home or set off on a journey. A catch phrase of the 20th century.

one of those days see **it's (just) one of those days.**

one sniff at the barmaid's apron and he's away see **he's had a smell of the barman's apron.**

one that got away, the applied to one who has providentially escaped some great danger, such as death or (in jocular usage) marriage. Since around 1945. From the use of the phrase by anglers boasting about the fish that escaped, oddly remarkable for its size or speed or cunning and by extension, for example, by a businessperson talking about a lucrative contract he/she has just failed to get.

only here for the beer, I'm (or **we're**, etc.) I've only come for a bit of fun (or, more literally, to take advantage of free drinks, etc.); said by one who has no serious interest in what is going on, no intention of participating, helping, etc., or perhaps not even any right to be there. The phrase originated in 1971 as an advertising slogan for Double Diamond beer.

only in the mating season see **do you come here often?**

only when I laugh the traditional response to the question 'Does it hurt?' given stoically by one who has suffered an injury, undergone a surgical operation, etc. Since around 1950 it has been used as a catch phrase in a wider range of contexts, often ironically, and has been popularized as the title of a novel by Len Deighton (1968), a film, and a television comedy series (first broadcast in 1979). (In the title of Deighton's novel, and sometimes elsewhere, the word *laugh* is spelt *larf*.)

ooh, you are awful(, but I like you)!   see **you are awful(, but I like you)!**

oompah, oompah, stick it up your jumper!   an expression of contempt, defiance, rejection or dismissal; perhaps originally a meaningless jingle chanted jocularly or derisively. The phrase dates from the 1920s. The word *oompah* is imitative of the sound of a trumpet, trombone or other brass instrument.

out of this world   exceedingly good, as in *his strawberry soufflé is out of this world*; an elaboration of the adjective 'heavenly' used as a term of approbation. The phrase was originally used by jazz musicians in the 1930s.

out to lunch   describes somebody who is either extremely eccentric or plain mad, as in *he's* (or *she's*) *out to lunch*. Later 20th century.

overpaid, over-sexed and over here   applied by the British to the GIs stationed in the UK during the latter part of World War II. The Americans' counter catch phrase was *you're underpaid, under-sexed and under Eisenhower*. (Eisenhower was the Supreme Commander of Allied Forces in Europe at the time.)

'owzat! (or **'owsat!**)   a general plea for recognition and acclamation, made by one who has just executed a neat or skilful action. Since around 1950. It is a contraction of *how's that?*, an appeal from the wicketkeeper to the umpire in cricket, meaning 'is the batsman out?'

P

paddle your own canoe! an exhortation to self-reliance. Popularized in the latter half of the 19th century by a music-hall song, the phrase may be derived from Frederick Marryat's *Settlers in Canada* (1844): 'I think it much better as we all go along together that every man paddle his own canoe.' It gave rise to the mock-French phrase *pas d'elle yeux Rhône que nous*, current during Partridge's schooldays in the early 20th century.

panic stations! used jocularly, for example, when something goes wrong, when something has to be done quickly, etc., as in *panic stations! I've lost my car keys!*; *the inspector will be here in half an hour – panic stations!* Since around 1939.

par for the course, that's about see **that's about par for the course**.

pardon me for living! said mock-apologetically by one who has been rebuked for some minor error or offence. The phrase occurs in Noël Coward's story 'A Richer Dust' in *Star Quality* (1951): 'He . . . said in a voice of bored petulance, "Lay off me for one minute, can't you." Discouraged, she withdrew her hand as requested, muttered "Pardon me for living", and took a swig of tomato juice.' A variant of the phrase has *breathing* in place of *living*.

pardon my French! please excuse the strong language!, as in *it's just another management fuck-up, (if you'll) pardon my French!* The phrase dates from around 1916. A chiefly US variant is *excuse my French!*

pas devant les enfants (or ***domestiques***) see **not in front of the children!**

patter of tiny feet, the a satirical reference to the joys or imminence of parenthood, as in *it's a popular misconception that all women yearn for the patter of tiny feet*. Since the 1920s. From Longfellow's poem *The Children's Hour*: 'I hear in the chamber above me / The patter of little feet.'

pay up and look pleasant refers to the payment of a statutory or otherwise unavoidable sum of money, such as a tax or the bill for something essential. The phrase dates from the mid-1940s in this form; earlier and later variants have other adjectives in place of *pleasant*. Perhaps suggested by the cliché *grin and bear it*.

peel me a grape an expression of cool or dismissive lack of concern.

It is one of a number of catch phrases associated with the US actress Mae West – in the film *I'm No Angel* (1933), after an enraged admirer has stormed out, she turns to her maid with a shrug and says: 'Beulah, peel me a grape.' (The phrase may have originated in the play *Diamond Lil* (1928).)

penny has dropped, the said by or of somebody who belatedly understands what was meant, or who gets the joke at last, as in *ah, the penny's dropped!* The phrase probably dates from the early 20th century. Perhaps from coin-operated devices, such as telephones, slot machines in an amusement arcade, the latches of public conveniences, etc., especially those that need a jog to make them work. See also **has the penny dropped?**

phantom . . . strikes again!, the applied to (or scrawled by the perpetrator of) any recurrent horror, e.g. a series of murders, robberies, acts of vandalism, poison-pen letters, etc., as in *the phantom cat-thief strikes again!* The phrase is often used in less serious contexts, e.g. by a practical joker or with reference to any sequence of similar incidents. Since the 1920s. Perhaps from (the title of) a film or book. See also **. . . rides again!**

pick on somebody your own size! i.e. pick a quarrel or fight with . . .. The phrase may be addressed to somebody who is bigger than the victim or (jocularly or derisively) to somebody smaller. Late 19th–20th centuries.

pin back your lug-holes (or **lug'oles**)! listen!; a catch phrase of the British entertainer Cyril Fletcher, who used it (from the 1940s or 1950s) before reciting one of his 'Odd Odes'. The word *lug-hole* is, of course, a slang term meaning 'ear'.

pip, pip! goodbye!; a cheery or jocular valediction. Since around 1915 or earlier. Variants include *toodle-oo pip-pip!* and *toodle-pip!* Perhaps imitative of the sound of an early motor-horn.

piss, or get off the pot! see **shit, or get off the pot!**

pissed (up)on from a great height, he should be (or **deserves to be**) he is beneath contempt; he should be reprimanded by somebody in much higher authority. (A less polite version has *shat* in place of *pissed*.) The phrase may be used in other persons and forms, as in *you deserve to be shat upon from a great height; I shall probably be pissed on from a great height*. It originated in the armed forces during World War II.

play it again, Sam! encore! This catch phrase is one of the most famous misquotations of all time – it is attributed to Humphrey Bogart in the film *Casablanca* (1942), but his actual words were: 'You played it for her, and you can play it for me. . . . Play it!' (Earlier in the film Ingrid Bergman had said: 'Play it once, Sam, for old time's sake. . . . Play it, Sam. Play *As Time Goes By*.') The phrase was used by Woody Allen as the title of a film (1972) featuring the ghost of Humphrey Bogart.

plot thickens, the things are becoming more complicated; used jocularly or ironically as a catch phrase since the late 19th century. The phrase probably derives from George Villiers, 2nd Duke of Buckingham's comedy *The Rehearsal* (1671): 'Ay, now the plot thickens very much upon us.'

poet and don't know it, you're (or **I'm**) **a** see **that's a rhyme if you take it in time**.

POETS short for 'piss off early, tomorrow's Saturday' (a more polite version has *push* in place of *piss*); used by those who work shorter hours (officially or unofficially) on Friday, which is thus known as *POETS day*. The acronym may have originated in the armed forces around 1960. See also **TGIF**.

point Percy at the porcelain a masculine reference to the act of urination, as in *I must just go and point Percy at the porcelain*. An Australianism introduced into the UK by the humorist Barry Humphries via the 'Barry McKenzie' comic-strip in the satirical magazine *Private Eye*. The phrase became particularly popular in the early 1970s.

point taken I accept your point (in an argument or discussion); also used as an acquiescent response to a justified rebuke, as in *point taken! It won't happen again, I promise*. Probably since the 1940s.

poor chap, he hasn't got two yachts to rub together said of a rich man complaining of his poverty. The phrase dates from the late 1960s. A variant substitutes *Rolls-Royces* for *yachts*; a similar phrase is *poor devil – down to his last million* (or *last yacht*).

pork chop in a synagogue used in similes for something that is embarrassingly out of place, extremely unpopular or unwelcome, etc., as in *the suggestion went down like a pork chop in a synagogue*, *as popular* (or *welcome*) *as a pork chop in a synagogue*. (Pork is, of course, forbidden to Jews.) Since around 1950.

pox-doctor's clerk, like a see **all dressed up like a Christmas tree**.

promises, promises! a jocular, sarcastic or defiant response to any appropriate remark, as in *'I'll swing for you one of these days!' 'Promises, promises!'* A catch phrase of the later 20th century. See also **is that a threat or a promise?**

protocol, alcohol and geritol a summary of the diplomatic life for an ageing man. (Geritol is a tonic.) A catch phrase attributed to the US politician and diplomat Adlai Stevenson during his time as ambassador to the United Nations (1961–5).

public enemy number one   applied to anybody who is particularly unpopular or undesirable, as in *the prime minister is public enemy number
one in this part of the country*. The phrase was originally applied to the
US gangster and outlaw John Dillinger, shot dead by FBI agents in
1934; it was adopted in the UK after World War II.

pull the other one (or **leg**) – **it's got bells on it!**   an   exclamation   of
disbelief. Since the 1920s or earlier. From the phrase *to pull (sb's) leg*,
to tease or fool (sb), with a probable allusion to the bells of a court
jester. See also **it's got bells on**.

pull your finger out!   get a move on!; get busy! The phrase probably
originated in the armed forces around 1930. Prince Philip, Duke of
Edinburgh, referred to it as a phrase he had 'picked up during the
war' when he used it in a speech about British industry on 17
October 1961: 'I think it is about time we pulled our fingers out.'
The word *pull* may be replaced by *take* or *get*; pompous, euphemistic
or learned variants include *dedigitate!*, *extract the manual digit!* and
extractum digitum! The phrase is probably an allusion to sexual
foreplay, delicately outlined by Kingsley Amis as follows: 'The full
reading is *take your finger out and get stuck in* and has to do with a
courting couple.'

pull your socks up!   try harder! Since around 1910. The phrase is also
used in other constructions, as in *she'd better pull her socks up if she
wants to pass this exam.*

put her (or **him**) **down, you don't know where she's** (or **he's**) **been**
jocularly addressed to one who is kissing or cuddling a member of
the opposite sex. The phrase been used in this way since the 1950s
or earlier. From the remark made by a hygiene-conscious parent to
a child who picks up and plays with a doll, ball or other toy found
in the street: 'Put it down, you don't know *where* it's been!'

put in a good word for me!   a jocular catch phrase addressed to a
person seen going to church on Sunday. Since the early 20th
century. A variant is *say one for me!*, which may also be addressed to
somebody kneeling (as if – but not – in prayer).

put it where the monkey put the nuts(, **you** (or **he, she**, etc.) **can**)   an
expression of refusal, rejection, etc., as in *tell him he can put it where the
monkey put the nuts!* Late 19th–20th centuries. Other verbs, notably
shove, may be used in place of *put*, and *puts its nuts* may be substituted
for *put the nuts*. The reference is, of course, anal (though it has been
pointed out that this is *not* where the monkey puts its nuts!). A similar
phrase is *you can put it where it will do the most good*. See also **if you don't
like it you can lump it!**; **you know what you can do with it.**

put up or shut up!   prove what you say (or back your assertion by

putting up money) or be silent. The phrase originated in the USA
in the late 19th century. In British usage it is often apprehended as
'put up your fists and fight, or shut up!' The phrase occurs in
Desmond Bagley's *Landslide* (1967); 'Now, put up or shut up. Do you
have anything to say? If not, you can get the hell out of here. . ..'

put your money where your mouth is!   back your words with cash. Used
in the USA since around 1930 and in the UK from around 1945.

Q

QED   short for *quod erat demonstrandum*; applied to something that was to be shown or proved, and now has been. A mathematical tag used jocularly as a catch phrase since the late 19th century, often with mock-pompous intonation and sometimes in the full form *quod erat demonstrandum*.

queer as Dick's hatband(, **as**)   very odd indeed. A phrase that originated in the mid-18th century and is still alive and well in northern England. Variants of the phrase include *as queer as Dick's hatband, that went round nine times and wouldn't meet* and *it's like Dick's hatband, that went round twice and wouldn't tie.* The identity of *Dick* is uncertain.

quick and dirty   applied to anything that is produced fast and without scrupulous accuracy, for example to meet a deadline or as a first draft. Used in the USA since before 1960; also used in the UK.

R

rather you than me! addressed, for example, to one who is about to embark on something that the speaker would find difficult or unpleasant, or that the speaker considers unlikely to succeed. Since around 1930. The phrase is also used in other persons, as in *'They're planning to cross the desert on foot.' 'Rather them than me!'*

read any good books lately? used as a social gambit in the 1920s and 1930s. (Less frequent variants include *seen any good plays* (or *films*) *lately?* and **have you heard any good stories lately?**) In *Much Binding in the Marsh* (a UK radio series of the late 1940s), Richard Murdoch popularized a slightly different use of the phrase: to change the subject in an awkward situation, for example when confronted by an embarrassing or unanswerable question, as in the following exchange between Kenneth Horne and Richard Murdoch: '"One of the nicest sandwiches I've ever had. What was it, Murdoch?" "Well, there was – er – have you read any good books lately?"' The phrase is still used for either purpose, jocularly or facetiously: a serious answer to the question is not expected.

read my lips used to emphasize what the speaker is about to say, which is often something that the person addressed seems unwilling or unable to hear, understand, believe or obey, as in *read my lips – we can't afford it!* (The words that follow the catch phrase are usually clearly articulated and heavily stressed, as if to facilitate lip-reading.) The phrase had already been in widespread use for many years when it was popularized in the nomination speech of the future US president George Bush (19 August 1988): 'Read my lips, no new taxes!' – a pledge that received far greater publicity when it was subsequently perceived to have been broken than when it was originally made. A frequent variant is *watch my lips*.

red hat and no knickers refers to ostentatious vulgarity in dress, with its implications of social or sexual vulgarity. Since around 1920. A similar phrase is *fur coat and no knickers*; variants of both phrases have *drawers* in place of *knickers*.

Reds under the bed applied to excessive suspicion of Communist influence, hence to any excessively suspicious attitude. The phrase originated in the USA, during Senator Joseph McCarthy's Communist witch-hunts of the 1950s, and soon reached the UK, where it became very common during the 1970s.

. . . refreshes the parts that other . . . cannot reach   used jocularly as a catch phrase, often with sexual innuendo. (Other verbs, notably *reaches*, may be substituted for *refreshes*.) From the slogan for Heineken lager, *Heineken refreshes the parts that other beers cannot reach*, used as the punch line or caption of a series of humorous advertisements since 1975.

remember the Alamo!   a chiefly jocular warning. The catch phrase alludes to the massacre by Mexican troops of a small US force at the Alamo (a mission in Texas) in 1836.

remember there's a war on!   see **don't you know there's a war on?**

rhubarb, rhubarb, rhubarb!   an elaboration of *rhubarb!*, meaning 'nonsense', derived from the mutterings of actors simulating the sound of background conversation, in crowd scenes, etc. Since around 1950.

ride 'em, cowboy!   a cry of encouragement, especially to somebody in a hazardous situation. The phrase originated in US rodeos of the 19th century in the form *ride 'er, cowboy!*, addressed to one taking part in the bronco-riding contest, the object of which was to stay on a bucking bronco (wild horse) for a full minute. It became a catch phrase in the 20th century.

. . . rides again!   used when somebody formerly famous comes back, after a long interval, in his or her well-remembered role, or when some hero or crusader effectually intervenes once again, especially in a spectacular manner. Any name or nickname may replace the ellipsis, but the two best-known examples are the film titles *Destry Rides Again* and *The Lone Ranger Rides Again*. The variant *. . . strikes again!* is usually applied to an antihero or villain; see also **phantom . . . strikes again!, the**.

right on!   that's exactly it!; that's fine!; an expression of agreement or approval. Used in the USA since the 1950s; also used in the UK.

right you are!   OK!; all right!; an expression of agreement or compliance. A catch phrase that dates from the mid-19th century.

rise and shine   an order to get out of bed. The phrase originated in the armed forces in the late 19th century. It is often followed (sometimes jocularly or ironically, e.g. before sunrise) by *the sun's burning a hole in your blanket, the sun will scorch your eyes out* (or *your balls off*), or a similar extension. See also **wakey, wakey!**

Roger the lodger   refers or alludes to a male lodger who has sexual intercourse with the mistress of the house. Since around 1925. The name *Roger* is used not only because it rhymes with *lodger*, but also because it is a pun on the slang verb *roger*, meaning 'copulate with'.

roll on, death!   may this monotony, this frustrating situation, this feeling of desperation, etc., come to an end!; said, for example, by a teacher or instructor whose pupils are slow to respond. The phrase is sometimes extended to . . . *and let's have a go* (or *a bash*) *at the angels.* The phrase probably originated in the armed forces during World War II.

roll on, duration!   a military catch phrase of 1917–18, expressing a fervent wish that the war might end soon. The use of the noun *duration* is derived from the fact that the volunteers of 1914–15 enlisted for three years or the duration of the war. The phrase *roll on, . . .* may be applied to any event that is eagerly anticipated or impatiently awaited, as in *roll on, pay-day!*

rolling in the aisles   see **I had 'em rolling in the aisles.**

run it up the flagpole (and see who salutes), let's   see **let's run it up the flagpole (and see who salutes).**

run that (one) by me again   means 'please repeat that' or 'give me another chance'. The phrase probably originated in the USA in the 1960s, when television re-runs and instant replays were developed.

rushing around like a blue-arsed fly   said by or of one who is rushing around in a frenzy, e.g. trying to complete a task before a deadline or to do several things at once, as in *I've been rushing around like a blue-arsed fly all morning.* 20th century. There is sometimes an implication of ineffectuality, like that of a bluebottle dashing itself against closed windows and other obstacles. See also **like a fart in a colander.**

S

safety in numbers(, **there's**)   used jocularly in sexual contexts, e.g. by somebody who does not want to be alone with a particular member of the opposite sex, or of a courting couple who cannot get up to anything while others are present. Late 19th–20th centuries. An extension of the proverbial use of the phrase.

said he (or **she**)   used by the speaker as a conventional tag, as in *'I'd love a cup of tea, said she hopefully.' 'No problem! I'll put the kettle on.'* Since the early 1920s.

same difference!(, **it's the**)   there is no difference – it's precisely the same thing; also used of things that are virtually or effectively the same, with the nuance 'don't expect me to share your pedantic concern for the distinction', as in *'They're French fries, not chips.' 'Same difference!'* The phrase has been in use since around 1940.

same here!   I agree; I think or feel the same as you do, as in *'I wish they'd put the prices on the goods, not on the shelves.' 'Same here!'* A 20th-century catch phrase of US origin.

same to you with (brass) knobs on!, the   means 'the same to you, only more so!'; said, for example, in response to an insulting remark. 20th century; often used by schoolchildren. The phrase may be a euphemism for the slang expression 'balls to you!'; it may also refer to the brass knobs on an old-fashioned bedstead. Variants include *the same to you with brass fittings* (chiefly US) and the more polite form *the same to you and many of them*, which dates from around 1880 or earlier. See also **with knobs on**.

san fairy Ann   it doesn't matter; it's all the same; it's not important; why worry? Since the latter part of World War I. A jocular corruption of the French phrase *ça ne fait rien*, meaning 'it doesn't matter'.

sandman is coming, the   said to or of children beginning to rub their eyes and yawn towards bedtime. The phrase dates from around 1850. An allusion to the effect of sprinkling sand in the eyes.

save the last dance for me   usually refers to sexual intercourse. The song of the same name, recorded by the Drifters in the late 1950s, contains the lines: 'But don't forget who's taking you home / And in whose arms you gonna be. / So, darling, save the last dance for me.' A variant of the phrase has *waltz* in place of *dance*.

saved by the bell said by or of one who is saved or spared at the last moment by a lucky accident or intervention. Late 19th–20th centuries. From boxing, where the bell indicates the end of each round.

say cheese! see **watch the dicky bird!**

say hey! an exclamation of excitement. The phrase originated in the USA in the 1950s or 1960s: the baseball player Willie Mays, who frequently used the expression, was nicknamed 'the *Say Hey* Kid'.

say it, don't spray it! see **spray it again, will you?**

say it with flowers! say it nicely! Since the 1920s. From a slogan coined in the US by Henry Penn, chairman of the National Publicity Committee of the Sociey of American Florists.

say no more! nothing more needs to be said – I understand, I am convinced, etc. See also **nudge, nudge, wink, wink!**

say one for me! see **put in a good word for me!**

say *something*, even if it's only goodbye! an exhortation to one who does not reply to the speaker's questions; usually delivered in a mock-pathetic tone and with an expression of wistful appeal. Possibly since the early 20th century.

say what? what was that you just said?; did you really say what I think you said? A chiefly US catch phrase that dates from the mid-1970s. See also **you what?**

says who? who says so?; usually uttered in a truculent or sarcastic tone of voice, with the implication 'I don't believe it!' Since the early 1930s. The phrase occurs with its standard response in the following quotation from Clarence B. Kelland's novel *Dreamland* (1938): '"Miss Higgs, you are guilty of reprehensible waste." "Says who?" "Says me," retorted Hadrian.' See also **sez you!**

says you! see **sez you!**

scout's honour! honestly!; you can take my word for it. Since around 1910; often jocular in modern usage. The phrase is based on the assumption that a Boy Scout would not lie on oath. See also **honest Injun!**

screw and bolt see **fuck 'em and chuck 'em**.

search me! means 'I don't know' or 'I have no idea' (i.e. you can search me but you won't find the answer), as in *What do you call a person who collects postcards?' 'Search me!'* The phrase originated in the USA around 1900 and was adopted in the UK around 1910.

see a man about a dog, I have (or I've got) to said when excusing oneself to go to the lavatory (or elsewhere), or in answer to the question 'Where are you going?' A catch phrase of the late 19th–20th centuries. In the USA around 1920 it had the specific meaning 'I must go out and buy some liquor.'

see you! I'll be seeing you; goodbye (for now). Used in the UK since the late 1930s. The phrase is sometimes met with the jocular response *not if I see you first!* Variants include *see you soon!* and *see you later!* (see also **see you later, alligator!**). See also **be seeing you!**

see you around! a valedictory catch phrase, sometimes a deliberately vague euphemism for a final goodbye (especially between former lovers, boyfriend/girlfriend, etc.). The phrase dates from around 1930.

see you in court! (, **I'll**) a jocular or ironic valediction. Since around 1910. Variants include *(I'll) see you in jail* and *(I'll) see you at the assizes.*

see you later, alligator! a valedictory catch phrase, to which the standard response is *in a while, crocodile.* The phrase was in vogue, especially among young people, in the 1950s and 1960s, popularized by a Bill Haley song in the film *Rock Around the Clock* (1956).

see you under the clock! refers to an agreed meeting soon to take place, but not necessarily under any particular clock. Probably adopted from US servicemen during the latter part of World War II.

seen any good plays (or **films**) **lately?** see **read any good books lately?**

sell in May and go away a catch phrase of the stock market, dating from the time when share prices were thought to drop in the holiday season for lack of investors: one could sell in May, go away for a long holiday (e.g. to the south of France) and buy at lower prices on one's return. The phrase originated during the inter-war years of 1919–39.

send for the marines! used when help is needed urgently. The phrase refers to assistance of any sort, not necessarily military aid. Since the 1940s or earlier.

separate the men from the boys, that'll (or **this'll**) refers to any situation (e.g. a crisis or emergency, or a test of courage, stamina, strength, etc.) that will serve to determine which are the 'real' men. Used in the USA since around 1930 and in the UK since the late 1930s. Variants include *that'll sort out the men from the boys* and *this is where the men are separated from the boys.*

sex rears its ugly head used whenever sex becomes an issue, e.g. when it is found to be the cause of a problem, or when it occurs intrusively in advertising, television programmes, books, etc. The phrase may have originated in an editorial by James R. Quirk in *Photoplay* magazine, concerning the US film *Hell's Angels* (1930). It occurs in Margery Allingham's *Flowers for the Judge* (1936): 'Once sex rears its ugly 'ead it's time to steer clear.'

sez you! an expression of doubt, scepticism or disbelief; often used derisively or belligerently to challenge the authority, knowledge or opinion of the person addressed, as in *'It was an accident.' 'Sez you!'*; *'It's impossible.' 'Sez you!'* Used in the USA since before 1925 and in the UK from around 1930. See also **says who?**

shake hands with the wife's best friend, I must go and   a masculine reference to the act of urination; said by a man excusing himself to go to the lavatory. Since around 1930 or earlier. The phrase also occurs in other forms, as in *'Where are you off to?' 'I'm just going to shake hands with the wife's best friend.'* A variant is . . . *shake hands with a very old friend*, which leads to the ritual exchange: *'Known him long?' 'I've known him longer!'*

shake the lead out of your ass!   get a move on! Used in the USA and Canada since around 1930; in British usage *arse* is sometimes substituted for *ass*. See also **get the lead out of your pants!**

shall we dance?   said by two people dodging in a doorway, narrow corridor, etc., each uncertain of which side to pass the other. Perhaps prompted or popularized by the song of this title from the highly successful musical *The King and I* (1956).

shan't play!   see **I shan't play!**

shape up or ship out!   a threat to get rid of the person addressed unless his or her work, performance, behaviour, etc., improves. The phrase originated in the armed forces during World War II; in civilian usage it is used, for example, by employer to employee.

shat (up)on from a great height, he should be (or **deserves to be**) see **pissed (up)on from a great height, he should be** (or **deserves to be**).

she bangs like a shithouse door   see **bangs like a shithouse door**.

she has seen something nasty in the woodshed   see **he** (or **she**) **has seen something nasty in the woodshed.**

she hasn't had it so long   a stock reply to the oft-heard complaint 'What has *she* got that *I* haven't (got)'; sometimes in the form *nothing, but she hasn't had it so long.* Since the 1940s.

'she' is the cat's mother (or **grandmother**)   usually addressed to a child who refers to his or her mother (or any other female) as 'she'. Since the mid-19th century or earlier. The phrase occurs in Dodie Smith's play *Touch Wood* (1934): '"Perhaps she'd play." "In my young days I was taught that 'she' was the cat's grandmother."' The variant *who's 'she' – the cat's mother* (or *grandmother*)? dates from the late 19th century.

she thinks the sun shines out of (sb's) arsehole   see **thinks the sun shines out of (sb's) arsehole, he** (or **she**).

she walks like she's got a feather up her ass   applied to a woman with a conspicuously self-conscious, mincing gait. A 20th-century catch phrase of Canadian origin; also used in the UK (with the vulgar variant *she walks like she's still got it in*). A variant used in the southern USA is *she walks like she's got a corncob up her cunt.*

she wants the whole world, with a little red fence around it   a jocular or cynical comment upon pre-marital feminine ambition. Mainly used in the USA, possibly since the 1920s. A variant is *he promised her the world, with a little red fence around it.*

she'd take you in, and blow you out again in little bubbles   deflatingly addressed to a male who boasts of his amorous or sexual designs on the female concerned; also used with reference to a particularly large and well-built woman. 20th century.

she'll be apples   see **apples, she's** (or **she'll be**).

she'll be right!   see **she's right!**

she'll die wondering   refers to an elderly virgin. A chiefly Australian catch phrase of the 20th century. Hence the phrase *at least she won't die wondering,* applied (since around 1920) to a woman who marries late and badly.

she's apples   see **apples, she's** (or **she'll be**).

she's got a bun in the oven   see **she's joined the club**.

she's got legs (right) up to her bum   used appreciatively by males of females, especially a long-legged female in a short skirt. Since the mid-19th century. The phrase also occurs in other forms, as in *a blue-eyed blonde with legs right up to her bum.*

she's got round heels   applied to a sexually compliant female, her heels being so round that the slightest nudge will put her on her back. A chiefly Canadian catch phrase that dates from around 1925.

she's joined the club   she is pregnant; applied especially to an unmarried girl or young woman. (This somewhat non-exclusive club is the *pudding club,* which dates from the late 19th century.) The synonymous phrase *she's got a bun in the oven* may be applied to any pregnancy, inside or outside marriage.

she's right!   that's all right!; don't mention it! The phrase is also used in the same way as *she's apples* (see **apples, she's** (or **she'll**) **be**), meaning 'all is well', with the variant *she'll be right!,* meaning 'all will be well'. Used in Australia and New Zealand since around 1925 or earlier. The use of *she* in this context may derive from its use with reference to ships and boats.

shit hits the fan, the   refers to the grave consequences of some action, as in *I don't want to be there when the shit hits the fan; wait till the boss hears about this – then the shit'll hit the fan!* Used in the USA and Canada since around 1930 and subsequently adopted in the UK. The phrase may have originated as an allusion to the agricultural muck-spreader.

shit off a shovel, (move) like get a move on!; move! (into position, etc.). The phrase probably originated in the armed forces before World War II.

shit, or get off the pot! get on with the job, or get out of the way and let somebody else (try to) do it!; also used in the simpler sense of 'make up your mind!' Of US origin, the phrase was adopted in the UK around 1944. A variant substitutes *piss* for *shit*, in order to make the phrase more alliterative and/or marginally less vulgar: this variant is probably more frequent in modern usage. See also **fish, or cut bait!**

shit out of luck in an extremely unfortunate position. Sometimes abbreviated to *SOL*. Used in the USA since the 1940s or earlier; also used in the UK.

shooting fish in a barrel, it's like see **it's like shooting fish in a barrel.**

shouldn't happen to a dog!, it (or **that**) see **it shouldn't happen to a dog!**

shove it where the monkey shoved the nuts(, **you** (or **he, she,** etc.) **can**) see **put it where the monkey put the nuts.**

shoving money upstairs refers to a suggested cause of baldness, perhaps alluding to the money spent on useless 'remedies' for this condition. A catch phrase of the 20th century.

show a leg! get out of bed! The phrase is of nautical (especially naval) origin and dates from the early 19th century. It was originally a call to show a leg from under the bedclothes, used to ascertain whether the occupant of the bed was male or female.

show must go on, the a traditional slogan or motto of the theatre, used whenever misfortune, illness, accident or disaster threatens to disrupt a performance or prevent it from taking place. See also **on with the motley!**

shut your eyes and think of England! see **close your eyes and think of England!**

sign of a misspent youth, the a comment upon anyone displaying proficiency at billiards or snooker. Since around 1930 or earlier.

since Pontius was a pilot since a very long time ago, as in *he's been with that mob since Pontius was a pilot.* The phrase is, of course, a pun on the name of *Pontius Pilate.* It originated in the RAF around 1944.

sir, you are speaking of the woman I love a cliché of 19th-century melodrama, used jocularly as a catch phrase since around 1890.

sit down, you're rocking the boat see **don't rock the boat!**

sitting by (or **with**) **Nellie** refers to the process of learning by observation from one who is competent and experienced. The phrase originated in the song 'On Mother Kelly's Doorstep'; it was formerly popular in northern mill towns, and has been in fairly general use since around 1960 (or earlier) for any in-service training.

sky's the limit, the   there is no limit or restriction; used with reference to money, opportunity, achievement, etc., as in *the minimum is £100, but the sky's the limit; for an ambitious young executive, the sky's the limit.* The phrase originated in the USA as a gambling term, referring to the size of a bet, in the early 20th century.

slaving over a hot stove all day   see **here am I, slaving over a hot stove all day**.

sleep tight! mind the fleas (or **bugs**) **don't bite!**   said at bedtime, usually to or by a child, but also jocularly among adults. Since the late 19th century or earlier. The full form of the phrase is *goodnight* (or *'night, 'night*), *sleep tight! . . .*; variants of the second part of the rhyme include *mind the bugs and fleas don't bite!* and *don't let the bedbugs bite!*

slice of the action, a   a share in (the equity, profits, etc., of) a venture, as in *I want a slice of the action; everybody wants a slice of the action*. Chiefly used in the business world in the later 20th century.

snafu   short for 'situation normal, all fucked up' (a more polite version has *fouled* in place of *fucked*). The acronym originated in the British armed forces during World War II. There are numerous similar phrases, including *FUBAR* (= fucked up beyond all recognition) and *SAPFU* (= surpassing all previous fuck-ups).

snake in your pocket?, have you got a   see **have you got a snake in your pocket?**

snowball's chance in hell, a   no chance at all. Late 19th–20th centuries. The phrase originated as *as much chance as a snowball in hell.* The word *snowball* may be replaced by *snowflake*. See also **not a cat in hell's chance**.

so fast his (or **her, your**, etc.) **feet won't touch (the ground)**   (the last two words are usually understood and omitted) very quickly indeed; in no time at all; usually refers to punishment for some misdemeanour, as in *if he gets caught they'll have him inside so fast his feet won't touch; any more of that and you'll be up before the CO so fast your feet won't touch.* The phrase originated in the armed forces and may date back to the late 19th century.

so stupid that he (or **she**) **can't chew gum and walk straight at the same time**   extremely stupid. Since around 1960. The phrase occurs in John Braine's *The Pious Agent* (1975): 'Not only is he so stupid that, to adopt a famous saying, he can't chew gum and walk straight at the same time, he's also illiterate.' It was popularized in the USA by a variant attributed to the former US president Lyndon Baines Johnson: 'Jerry Ford is so dumb he can't fart and chew gum at the same time.'

so sue me!   then do something about it! A chiefly US catch phrase that dates from the 1950s or earlier.

so what? that doesn't impress or interest me; what does it matter?, as in *'She's earning twice as much as you.' 'So what?'; 'He's been married before.' 'So what?'* Used in the USA since around 1930; adopted in the UK around 1936.

so what else is new? see **what else is new?**

sock it to me! a catch phrase that was popularized by the US television series *Rowan and Martin's Laugh-In* (first broadcast in 1967, also in the UK), in which the speaker (usually Judy Carne or one of the show's guests) suffered instant retribution in the form of a bucket of water over the head, a fall through a trapdoor, etc. The phrase is also used (with other personal pronouns in place of *me*) as a general cry of encouragement or provocation, as in *go on, sock it to him!* The idiom *to sock it to (sb)*, meaning 'to deliver a devastating blow, literally or figuratively' (from the slang verb *sock*, meaning 'hit'), occurs in Mark Twain's *A Connecticut Yankee in the Court of King Arthur* (1889): 'I prepared, now, to sock it to him. I said: "Look here, dear friend, ..."' It was subsequently used with sexual connotations, as in *I'd like to sock it to* her*!*, and in the sense of 'speak forcefully or impressively', as in *you should have heard him – he really socked it to them!*

soft as shit and twice as nasty, as applied by rustics, especially in south-east England, to urban owners of weekend cottages in the country. Late 19th–20th centuries.

softly, softly, catchee monkey gently does it! Late 19th–20th centuries. Often used with reference to the apprehension of criminals, the phrase was adopted as the motto of the Lancashire Constabulary Training School and inspired the title of the television police drama series *Softly Softly* (first broadcast in 1966). It has also given rise to the attributive adjective *softly-softly*, meaning 'cautious; discreet; gradual', as in *a softly-softly approach*.

sold to the man (or **woman**) **in the . . .** it's yours; you've got it; that's perfectly correct. 20th century. From a phrase used at auctions, as in *sold to the gentleman in the bowler hat; sold to the lady in the red coat.*

some hope! there's little or no chance of that happening!; a pessimistic or discouraging remark or reply, as in *'He might change his mind.' 'Some hope!'* The phrase probably dates from around 1890. See also **I should be so lucky!**

some like it hot applied to jazz, sex, etc. The phrase is ultimately derived from the nursery rhyme *Pease Porridge Hot*: 'Some like it hot, / Some like it cold; / Some like it in the pot, / Nine days old.' Its popularity as a catch phrase dates from 1959, when it was used as the title of a highly successful film starring Marilyn Monroe, Jack

Lemmon, and Tony Curtis. (The same title had been used 20 years earlier for an unremarkable film starring Bob Hope.)

some mothers do 'ave (or **have**) **'em!** applied to any display of clumsiness, stupidity, etc. The phrase was used as the title of a television comedy series featuring the accident-prone Frank Spencer, played by Michael Crawford, first broadcast in 1974. In the form *don't some mothers have* (or *'ave*) *'em!* it was popularized from the late 1950s by Jimmy Clitheroe in the radio series *The Clitheroe Kid.*

some of my best friends are Jews I'm not prejudiced against Jews; often used to excuse or mitigate a remark that implies or indicates anti-Semitism, or in protest at such a remark made by another. Probably since the 1930s. In modern usage the phrase is often used jocularly or ironically, and the name of any minority group, class, profession, nationality, race, religion, etc., may be substituted for *Jews,* as in *some of my best friends are vegetarians* (or *estate agents, Australian, Catholic,* etc.).

some say . . . – others (or **I**) **say . . .** used to introduce a contradiction, as in *some say good old Frobisher – I say fuck old Frobisher!* Of military origin, the phrase has been in general use since around 1919. The second part of the phrase is sometimes replaced by *others tell the truth.*

somebody up there likes me (or **you**) said by (or to) one who has had a stroke of good fortune, a narrow escape, etc. (In this sense 'somebody up there' refers to God or some other heavenly being.) The phrase is also used less figuratively by (or to) one who seems to be in favour with those in authority. Popularized in the USA as the title of a film (1956) starring Paul Newman, it was adopted as a catch phrase in the UK around 1960.

something is rotten in the state of Denmark refers to corruption, especially social or political corruption. It has been suggested that this famous quotation from Shakespeare's *Hamlet* may have already been a catch phrase in the late 16th century. The line is often misquoted as *there's something rotten in the state of Denmark.*

something nasty in the woodshed, he (or **she**) **has seen** see **he** (or **she**) **has seen something nasty in the woodshed.**

sometimes I wonder! elliptical for 'sometimes I wonder whether you are entirely sane, right in the head, etc.'; prompted by a particularly stupid remark or foolish action. The phrase is usually delivered in a reflective tone of voice, accompanied by a sigh of exasperation, a puzzled shaking of the head, etc. A catch phrase of the 20th century.

sort out the men from the boys, that'll see **separate the men from the boys, that'll** (or **this'll**).

spare my blushes! a response to an embarrassingly flattering statement or compliment; often used jocularly or ironically. The phrase dates from around 1880.

sparrows flying out of one's backside, like   see **like sparrows** (or **geese**) **flying out of one's backside.**

speak softly and carry a big stick   a catch phrase popularized in the early 20th century by Theodore Roosevelt, in a speech he made during his presidency of the USA: 'There is a homely adage which runs "Speak softly and carry a big stick; you will go far."'

spell it out for you?, do I have to   see **do I have to spell it out for you?**

spending money as if it were going out of fashion   spending money recklessly, as if it were soon to become worthless. Since around 1930. A chiefly US variant has *style* in place of *fashion*. See also **like there was no tomorrow.**

spot on!   exactly right, as in *'I reckon she's a retired headmistress.' 'Spot on!'* The phrase originated in the RAF during World War II, meaning 'dead centre on target', and subsequently entered civilian usage.

spray it again, will you?   said to somebody who accidentally spits while talking (e.g. when articulating the letters *p, s, sp,* etc.). Used in Australia since the 1940s; also used in the UK. A variant is *spray it again, Sam!* (a pun on **play it again, Sam!**); similar phrases include *say it, don't spray it!* and *you can spray that again!* (a pun on **you can say that again!**).

squeeze till the pips squeak   to extract the utmost from. In its original context (a speech made by Sir Eric Geddes on 10 December 1918) the phrase referred to obtaining reparations from Germany after World War I: 'The Germans . . . are going to pay every penny; they are going to be squeezed as a lemon is squeezed – until the pips squeak.' In modern usage the phrase is most frequently applied to taxation of the wealthy; it may also refer to the extraction of information.

stand by to repel boarders!   used jocularly when visitors approach or arrive – the visitors may be welcome or unwelcome, expected or unexpected. A 20th-century catch phrase of naval origin.

stand up and be counted!   show your true political colours, religious beliefs, support for a cause, etc.; make known your views, opinions, attitude, etc., as in *it's time for the opponents of European unity to stand up and be counted.* Since around 1920.

steal anything that's not too hot or too heavy, he'd (or **she'd**, etc.) applied to a notoriously light-fingered person. The general form of this phrase has been traced back to Chaucer. Variants include *he'd steal anything that isn't nailed down* and (of somebody particularly unscrupulous and dishonest) *he'd steal the pennies off a dead man's eyes* or *he'd steal the grace out of the Hail Mary.*

step outside and say that! a threat of violence, in response to an offensive remark. The phrase is often jocular in modern usage. It originated in the USA in the early 20th century and was subsequently adopted in the UK.

sticks like shit to a blanket, he (or **she**) refers to somebody who is hard to get rid of. The phrase has been in widespread use throughout the UK (and elsewhere) for many years. The variant *it sticks* (or *clings*) *like shit to a blanket* is applied to any viscous, sticky, clinging substance.

stop me if you've heard it (or **this one**) a stock preamble to a joke or anecdote. Since the 1920s. A story of the same name in Noël Coward's *Star Quality* (1951) contains the following trenchant comment: 'That idiotic insincere phrase – that false, unconvincing opening gambit – as though people ever had the courage to stop anyone however many times they've heard it.'

stop the world, I want to get off I'm tired of life; said only half-seriously, not in genuine despair. The phrase originated as the title of a musical by Anthony Newley and Leslie Bricusse, first performed in 1961.

stopped the show, he (or **she**) applied to a brilliant actor, singer, dancer, etc. Probably since the 1920s. The phrase literally refers to one whose performance draws such acclamation from the audience that the show comes to a temporary halt; the idiom *to stop the show* may also be used of a line, joke, song, etc.

story of my life!, (that's) the an expression of rueful resignation used (with a spark of humour not entirely quenched by pessimism) in response to any setback, disappointment, failure, etc. – often something that has happened before, especially frequently, or that the speaker considers typical of his or her customary ill fortune. Later 20th century. See the quotation from the 'Peanuts' strip-cartoon at **low man on a** (or **the**) **totem pole**.

strong, silent type, (a or **the)** originally a cliché of romantic fiction, applied to a man who says little but does much; used sarcastically or derisively as a catch phrase since the early 1920s, perhaps from the realization among intelligent women that such men can be pretty dull to live with. See also **tall, dark and handsome**.

suck it and see! try it out!, as in *'Do you think it will work?' 'Who knows? Suck it and see!'* The phrase dates from the 1890s and may be of music-hall origin. It has also been used as a derisive retort, chiefly by children in the 1930s–50s.

sucking (on) the hind tit applied to anybody who gets the most unfavourable draw, especially in horse-racing, or who comes in late, in last place, etc. A catch phrase of the 20th century.

sure thing! certainly!; an emphatic affirmative response to a direct question or an implied doubt. The phrase has been used in the USA since the late 19th century and in the UK from 1910 or earlier.

surprise me! show me how intelligent, original, etc., you are!; often used sarcastically. Adopted from the USA in the 1950s.

surprise! surprise! said, for example, by an unexpected visitor, or by anybody presenting another with a genuine (and usually welcome) surprise, as in *you thought I'd forgotten your birthday, didn't you? . . . Surprise! surprise!* The phrase is also used in the sense of 'what a surprise!', especially ironically by one who is not at all surprised, as in *I failed my driving test again – surprise! surprise!*; *'She phoned to say she can't come and help – one of her kids is ill.' 'Surprise! surprise!'*; *'Martin won.' 'Surprise! surprise!'* Probably since the 1950s.

surprised? you could have fucked me through my oilskins! chiefly used ironically, meaning 'I was not at all surprised'. The phrase is probably of naval origin, and may date back to World War I or earlier.

T

ta-ta for now! goodbye for now! The phrase is often abbreviated to *TTFN*, an acronym that was popularized in the 1940s by the character Mrs Mopp (played by Dorothy Summers) in the radio series *ITMA*. The variant *BFN*, short for *bye for now!*, has been in general use since the 1960s, when it became a catch phrase of the disc-jockey Jimmy Young.

take a running jump at yourself!(, **go and**) an exclamation of dismissal, refusal or rejection. A chiefly Canadian variant is *(go and) take a running fuck at the moon!* See also **go (and) jump in the lake!**

take all you want: take two! an expression of qualified generosity. Used in the USA since 1945 or earlier; also used in the UK. The phrase is probably Yiddish in origin, being used by Jews themselves in jocular self-mockery.

take me to your leader! a catch phrase used jocularly in any appropriate context. It probably originated in adventure stories of the 19th century (said, for example, by explorer to primitive tribesman); since around 1950 it has been widely used in science fiction (said, for example, by extra-terrestrial to earthling).

take your finger out! see **pull your finger out!**

talk about laugh! I (or we, etc.) really did laugh heartily, as in *you should've seen him trying to dance with his leg in plaster: talk about laugh!* Probably since around 1860. See also **laugh? I thought I should have died**.

tall, dark and handsome originally a cliché applied to the romantic hero of a novel, play, etc.; used ironically and derisively as a catch phrase since around 1910. See also **strong, silent type**.

tell it like it is tell it without the slightest elaboration or suppression of the truth; give the real facts; be honest, as in *come on, tell it like it is!*; *the tabloid newspapers claim to tell it like it is*. The phrase probably originated among US Blacks around 1960, and was subsequently associated with hippies and young people before entering general usage in the UK. It was used in a *Sunday Times* headline of 21 September 1977: 'State industry must tell it like it is.'

tell me another! I don't believe that!; an exclamation of amazement or incredulity. The phrase occurs in Alfred Sutro's comedy *Rude Min and Christine* (1915): "'I say, Minnie and I are going to get married.' "Go on! Tell me another!'"

tell me news (– that's ancient history)!   a response to stale news, an old story or joke, etc. Since the 18th century. See also **tell me something I don't know!**; **what else is new?**

tell me something I don't know!   I've known that for ages; that's common knowledge. Since the late 19th century. See also **tell me news . . .!**; **what else is new?**

tell that to the marines!   I don't believe that; you must think I'm a fool if you expect me to believe that; addressed, for example, to the teller of a tall story. The phrase originated in the early 19th century. The implication is that the marines are more credulous than other sailors: in 1823 Byron used the variant *that will do for the marines, but the sailors won't believe it.* Another variant (now obsolescent) is *tell that to the horse-marines!*

tell you what!   see **I'll tell you what!**

ten a penny   see **they're two (or ten) a penny**.

tennis, anyone?   see **anyone for tennis?**

TGIF   short for 'thank God it's Friday!' The abbreviation may have originated among primary- and secondary-school teachers in the first half of the 20th century; since around 1950 (at the latest) it has been used by anybody whose working week ends on Friday. See also **POETS**.

thank you for having me   see **thanks for having me**.

thank you for nothing! I owe you no thanks for that!; an ironic response to an unhelpful remark or action, a refusal or rejection, a disservice, etc. Since around 1910. A variant is *thanks for nothing!*

thank you for sharing that with us   an ironic comment upon somebody's unpleasant news, gruesome story, sick joke, etc. Since around 1960; chiefly used in the USA.

thank you for those few kind words   an expression of gratitude, said jocularly in response to a compliment (especially by one who has recently suffered much misfortune) or ironically in response to a backhanded compliment or an uncomplimentary remark. Since around 1910 or earlier. A less frequent variant of the phrase is *many thanks for those few kind words*.

thanks, but no thanks!   a polite, jocular or ironic refusal of an offer, e.g. of something that is undesirable or likely to do more harm than good, as in *'I could get you a job at the sausage factory.' 'Thanks, but no thanks!'*; *'Shall I send the kids over to give you a hand?' 'Thanks, but no thanks!'* Since around 1955.

thanks for having me   said (with ironic emphasis on the word *having*) by a departing guest to the landlady of a boarding-house. 20th century. The phrase *thank you* (or *thanks*) *for having me* is, of course, a conventional polite formula used by any departing guest (whether paying or not); in this context there is a pun on *having* in the sense of 'swindling'. The phrase is also used jocularly in other contexts with a pun on other senses of the verb (e.g. 'having sexual intercourse with').

thanks for nothing!   see **thank you for nothing!**

that adds up   see **it doesn't add up**.

that ain't hay!   see **and that ain't hay!**

that beats working   see **beats working**.

that makes two of us   me too (or me neither); I think, feel, etc., the same, as in *'I don't understand.' 'That makes two of us.'* Since around 1940 or earlier. See also **you and me both!**

that really rattled his (or **her**) **cage**   that upset him (or her) considerably. A catch phrase of the later 20th century, perhaps influenced by the colloquial use of the verb *rattle* in the sense of 'disconcert; fluster'. See also **who rattled your cage?**

that shook him (or **her**)!   that astounded, startled, perplexed, baffled, or greatly perturbed him (or her)! The phrase originated in the armed forces during World War II. An intensive variant is *that shook him* (or *her*) *rigid!*

that shouldn't happen to a dog!   see **it shouldn't happen to a dog!**

that takes the cake!   that beats everything!; an exclamation of indignant astonishment or incredulity, applied, for example, to an extremely impudent act or remark, a tall story, etc. Of US Black origin, the phrase originally referred to the cake awarded as a prize to the winner of a cakewalk (a contest that subsequently developed into the dance of this name); it was adopted in the UK around 1895. A variant is *that takes the biscuit!*

that was no lady: that was my wife   a stock response to any question along the lines of 'Who was that lady I saw you with last night?' The phrase probably originated as a music-hall joke in the 1880s or 1890s. It may also be used in the present tense, as in *'Who's that lady over there in the red dress?' 'That's no lady: that's my wife!'*

that went down like a lead balloon   see **went down like a lead balloon, it** (or **that**).

that won't wash!   that is unconvincing; that won't work, as in *that won't wash in a court of law, it's no use turning on the tears – that won't wash with me!* The phrase dates from around 1840 or earlier.

that would be telling!   a reply made by one who tauntingly withholds the desired information, as in *'Where did you find it?' 'That would be telling!'*; usually said in an irritatingly smug tone of voice, meaning 'I know something *you* don't know!' The phrase originated in the 19th century, when it often occurred in the variant form *that's telling(s)!* See also **that's for me to know and you to find out**.

that'll be the day   an ironic expression of extreme scepticism or incredulity, referring to something that is very unlikely to happen, as in *'She may offer to pay.' 'That'll be the day.'* Since around 1917 or earlier. The popularity of the phrase may have been reinforced by the rock-and-roll song of the same name, by Buddy Holly and the Crickets, which reached the top of the hit-parade in 1957 and was subsequently recorded by many other singers and groups; it was also used as the title of a film in 1973. The variant *that'll be the frosty Friday* is used in New Zealand (and possibly elsewhere). See also **it'll be a cold day in hell (when . . .)**.

that'll put lead in your pencil   that will render you potent, restore your virility, etc.; chiefly applied to food or drink, especially alcoholic liquor, offered after illness or to anybody displaying the merest semblance of sexual fatigue. Late 19th–20th centuries. See also **it'll put hair on your chest**.

that'll separate (or **sort out**) **the men from the boys**   see **separate the men from the boys, that'll** (or **this'll**).

that's a cinch   see **cinch, it's** (or **that's**) **a**.

that's a good question!   that's a very shrewd or pertinent question (sometimes used to gain time while the speaker seeks a suitable response); that's a very difficult question and I don't know the answer, as in *'How are we going to get out?' 'That's a good question!'* Since the mid-1940s. The phrase is often shortened to *good question!*; an intensive variant is *that's a very good question!* See also **that's the sixty-four thousand dollar question!**

that's a good 'un (or **one**)!   what a fib!, as in *twenty-five? That's a good 'un – she must be at least forty!* Originally applied to an excellent story, funny joke or witty remark, the phrase dates from around 1660 and occurs in Joseph Addison's comedy *The Drummer* (1716): 'Frightened with a drum! That's a good one!'

that's a hell of a note!   what a plight or predicament!; applied to a very grave or disastrous situation. Used in the USA from around 1930; occasionally used in the UK since around 1960. The phrase alludes to a (musical) note that is badly out of tune.

that's a hell of a way to run a railway (or **railroad**)!   see **what a way to run a railway** (or **railroad**)!

that's a horse of another (or **a different**) **colour**   that's quite another matter. Used in the USA since the 1790s and in the UK from around 1840. The phrase was probably suggested by a line from Shakespeare's *Twelfth Night*: 'My purpose is indeed a horse of that colour.' It is sometimes intensified by the addition of *quite* or *very*.

that's a load of old cobblers! that's utter nonsense; often shortened to *cobblers!* Since the late 1950s. The slang term *cobblers*, meaning 'nonsense; rubbish', is short for *cobbler's awls*, rhyming slang for *balls* (in the sense of 'testicles').

that's a new one on me see **new one on me, it's** (or **that's**) **a.**

that's a rhyme if you take it in time addressed to one who has said something that happens to rhyme, such as 'I'd go by car, but it's not that far'. The phrase dates from around 1700. A variant is *you're a poet and* (or *but*) *don't know it,* which is also used in other persons; the form *I'm a poet and don't* (or *didn't*) *know it,* for example, may be said by the person who has made the accidental rhyme, as in Ellery Queen's *The Last Woman in His Life* (1970): 'She can't hope to cope! I'm a poet and don't know it!'

that's a turn-up for the book! see **what a turn-up for the book!**

that's a very good question! see **that's a good question!**

that's a whole nother matter that's quite another matter. Chiefly used in the USA. This division of the word *another* to add emphasis seems to follow the pattern of the slang term *absobloodylutely*, an intensification of *absolutely*.

that's about par for the course that's normal, average or usual; that's what might be expected; often used ironically and/or pejoratively of a low standard of performance, as in *'It took them three months to reply to my letter.' 'That's about par for the course.'* Since around 1920. Paradoxically, in its original golfing context the phrase *par for the course* implies a high standard of performance, being the number of strokes that a good player should take, and is therefore *not* what might be expected of the average golfer.

that's about the size of it that's a fairly accurate description of the state of affairs; a cliché adopted from the USA around 1915. Since around 1920 it has also been used as a catch phrase with sexual innuendo, accompanied by a gesture in which the forearm is allowed to fall forward and down, the palm of the lightly-clenched fist uppermost.

that's all I need! that's the last straw!, as in *I'm already late, and now the bloody car won't start – that's all I need!* The phrase dates from around 1958 or earlier.

that's all she wrote that's all there is; it's finished. The phrase is of US origin; during World War II it referred to a 'dear John' letter – a soldier's last letter from his girlfriend, telling him that their relationship is over.

that's all water under the bridge see **water under the bridge, it's** (or **that's**) **all**.

that's another can of worms that's a different problem; usually said by one who is already dealing with a related or unrelated problem. The phrase *can of worms*, meaning 'extremely complex problem', has been current in the USA since the early 1940s and was adopted in the UK around 1977. It also occurs in such idioms as *to open a whole new can of worms*, referring to the introduction of additional complications into an already complicated situation.

that's anyone's bet see **anyone's bet**.

that's flat! see **and that's flat!**

that's for me to know and you to find out a catch phrase that is virtually synonymous with **that would be telling!**, used especially by children, as in *'Where is it?' 'That's for me to know and you to find out.'* 20th century; of US origin.

that's for the birds see **that's strictly for the birds**.

that's going some! that's going too far!; also used as an expression of admiration or approval. Adopted from the USA around 1910 or earlier.

that's life! that's the way things happen; applied to something undesirable but inevitable, which must be accepted, as in *I like him, but he doesn't like me – oh well, that's life, I suppose!* The phrase has been used since the mid-1970s as the title of British television series dealing with consumer issues, hosted by Esther Rantzen. The French form *c'est la vie!* is an occasional variant. See also **that's the way it goes**.

that's made my day see **made my day, you've** (or **that's** or **it's**).

that's mighty (or **damn**) **white of you!** that's very decent, generous, forgiving, obliging, etc., of you! Used in the USA from the early 20th century and the UK since the 1930s. The phrase may have originated in the southern USA (or in the colonies of the British Empire), with racist connotations; in modern usage it is addressed by everybody to anybody, often jocularly or ironically.

that's more like it! that's better!; that's more acceptable, reasonable, etc., as in *'Would you like a cup of tea? . . . How about a beer, then?' 'That's more like it!'* A catch phrase of the 20th century. See also **that's something like it!**

that's my boy! a variant of **attaboy!** This form of the phrase was popularized by the proud father bulldog boasting of his puppy son in a series of US film cartoons frequently shown on British television.

that's my story and I'm sticking to it that's my version of events, explanation, excuse, alibi, etc. – you can believe it or not; an assertion that one is telling the truth, sometimes used jocularly by one who is obviously lying or stubbornly by one who is unwilling to retract what he or she has said. Adopted from the USA in the mid-1930s, the phrase occurs in Noël Coward's play *Relative Values* (1951). Variants include . . . *and I'll stick to it* and . . . *and I'm stuck with it*, the latter being said ruefully by one who is unable to retract what he or she has said.

that's no lady: that's my wife see **that was no lady: that was my wife**.

that's not cricket! see **not cricket!, it's** (or **that's**).

that's not my department that's not my responsibility; said, for example, by one who wishes to pass the buck. The phrase has been used in the UK and the USA since the late 1940s.

that's one for the book see **one for the book**.

that's put the (tin) lid on it that's done it; that's finished it (especially in an unsatisfactory or unpleasant way); that's the last straw. A catch phrase of the late 19th–20th centuries. Variants have *tin hat* or *top hat* in place of *(tin) lid*.

that's showbiz for you! that's how it goes! The phrase originally referred to the ups and downs of the entertainment world, especially in the USA, but has had a wider application in the UK since the late 1930s. See also **that's the way it goes**.

that's something else (again) that's a (very) different matter; also used as an expression of high approbation. The phrase has been used (in the first sense) in the USA since the early 1930s and was adopted in the UK during World War II; the second sense is probably of Black origin.

that's something like it! that's as it should be; that's more pleasant, closer to what I had in mind, etc. Used in the USA since the 1920s and in the UK from the 1930s. See also **that's more like it!**

that's straight from central casting applied to something that is conventional or stereotyped, requiring no imagination. The phrase originated in the US film industry, becoming more widespread in the 1960s.

that's strictly bush applied to somebody whose behaviour is unmannerly. The phrase seems to have originated in the USA around 1905. It is probably derived from the term *busher*, denoting one who has not made the grade (originally a baseball player who did not make the 'Big League'), influenced by *bush* in the sense of 'backwoods', or the Australian bush.

that's strictly for the birds rubbish!; applied to something that is unbelievable, unacceptable, unwanted, worthless, etc. (The word *strictly* is sometimes omitted.) Adopted from the USA around 1955. The phrase may allude to horse manure, a source of nourishment for certain sectors of the bird population, especially in the days of horse-drawn vehicles.

that's that that is the end of the matter; often an expression of rueful resignation, as in *well, that's that – I don't suppose I'll ever see her again.* 20th century.

that's the name of the game that's what it's all about (see also **name of the game, the**). Since around 1965. The phrase occurs in Desmond Cory's *The Circe Complex* (1975): 'Ergonomics, baby. *That's* the name of the game.'

that's the sixty-four (thousand) dollar question! applied to a crucial, very puzzling, very difficult, or unanswerable question, as in *'Why didn't he tell the police?' 'That's the sixty-four thousand dollar question!'* The phrase originated in the USA as *that's the sixty-four dollar question,* which alluded to the highest prize of $64 in the radio quiz show *Take It or Leave It* (1941–8); in a subsequent US television game show the award was raised to $64,000. An early British television version, *Double Your Money,* was first broadcast in 1955 with a top prize of £64; however, the catch phrase was not adopted in the UK until the 1960s and remains in US dollars in British usage. See also **that's a good question!**

that's the stuff to give the troops! that's just what is wanted or needed; an expression of enthusiastic appreciation (especially of food or drink) or encouragement. This form of the phrase probably originated in the armed forces during World War I, but the shorter version *that's the stuff!* was current in the USA in the late 19th century and occurred in a music-hall song of around 1910.

that's the ticket! that's the best thing to do; that's right; that's what is required. The phrase probably dates from around 1820. It may have originated as an allusion to the winning ticket in a lottery, or to the ticket on an item of merchandise (as in the now-obsolete variant *that's the article!*).

that's the way it goes an expression of jocular resignation or rueful acceptance. Since the mid-19th century. Similar phrases include **that's life!, that's showbiz for you!, that's the way the ball bounces,** and **that's the way the cookie crumbles.**

that's the way the ball bounces a less common synonym of **that's the way the cookie crumbles.** Used in the USA since around 1954 and occasionally used in the UK.

that's the way the cookie crumbles that's how it has turned out, and there's nothing you can do about it; a philosophical comment on the perversity of fate, the arbitrariness of fortune, etc. The phrase has been in frequent use in the USA since the 1950s and was adopted in the UK in the mid-1960s. It occurs in Edward Albee's play *The Zoo Story* (1959): '"Well ... naturally, every man wants a son, but ..." "But that's the way the cookie crumbles?"' In Billy Wilder's film *The Apartment* (1960), the character played by Jack Lemmon says, 'That's the way it crumbles cookie-wise', neatly deriding both the phrase itself and the voguish overuse of the suffix *-wise*. Variants include **that's the way the ball bounces** and *that's the way the mop flops*; see also **that's the way it goes.**

that's the whole ball of wax   that's it; that's all there is to it; that's the nub of the matter. The phrase probably dates from the 1960s.

that's too bad!   used ironically, indicating a lack of concern or sympathy, especially for the wishes, needs or problems of others. This use of the phrase may have originated in the late 19th century. It occurs in Terence Rattigan's play *Love in Idleness* (1944): 'You dislike me, I dislike you. Well, that's too bad, but we needn't act like primeval apes about it.'

that's torn it!   that's ruined everything; said in response to a major or minor disaster, as in *the battery's gone flat – that's torn it!* Since around 1905. A US correspondent has suggested a sexual derivation, referring to the tearing of a condom (there may also be an allusion to the loss of virginity), but the phrase is probably of more mundane origin, e.g. the tearing of a garment.

that's what *you* think!   that's your opinion, but you're wrong!; often used derisively (e.g. by one who has information to the contrary) or defiantly (e.g. by one who intends to thwart the other's plans), as in *'You can't prove it.' 'That's what you think!'* A catch phrase of the 20th century.

that's where it's at   that's a fair or accurate view of things. Used in the USA since around 1964 and in the UK from around 1972. The slang phrase *where it's at* means 'the right, ideal, popular or fashionable place, situation, opinion, activity, etc.'

that's your best bet   that's the best way for you to do something, to get somewhere, etc., as in *why don't you drive to Dover and take the ferry from there – that's your best bet*. Since the 1920s. The phrase is also used in other persons and constructions, as in *his best bet would be to phone the hospital and ask their advice*.

that's your funeral   see **your funeral, it's** (or **that's**).

that's your lot!   see **and that's your lot!**

then the shit'll hit the fan   see **shit hits the fan, the.**

there ain't no justice!   an observation on the manifest inequalities and unfairness of life in general. The phrase dates from the mid-20th century or earlier.

there ain't no such animal I just don't believe it! Since around 1880. The phrase is believed to be of US anecdotal origin, having been said either by a rustic on seeing a giraffe for the first time or (according to *Bartlett's Familiar Quotations*) by a New Jersey farmer of a circus dromedary. There are a number of dialectal variants, notably *there ain't no sech animule* and *there ain't no sech critter.*

there ain't nobody here but us chickens! see **ain't nobody here but us chickens!**

there and back a response to the question 'Where are you going?'; often used among children. A catch phrase of the late 19th–20th centuries. The full form is *there and back to see how far it is.*

there are no flies on him (or **her**) see **no flies on him** (or **her**), **there are.**

there are no two ways about it see **there's no two ways about it.**

there are only a few of us left used jocularly or ironically as a catch phrase since around 1965. It occurs in Donald Mackenzie's *Postscript to a Dead Letter* (1973): 'Jean Paul's one . . . who knows that what he's done is good and doesn't bother to tell you. There are only a few of us left.' A variant is *there aren't many of us left*, as in *he was one of nature's gentlemen – there aren't many of us left.*

there are plenty more fish in the sea addressed consolingly to one whose romance has come to an end, especially to a girl jilted by her boyfriend. Since the early 20th century. A variant is *there are plenty more pebbles on the beach*; see also **you're not the only pebble on the beach.**

there he stood with his finger in his ass . . . wondering what on earth to do. Chiefly used in the USA, since the 1920s. A similar phrase, dating from the 1940s or earlier, is *with thumb in bum and mind in neutral*, applied to somebody who seems vacant, uninterested, etc.

there is always (a) tomorrow indicates that one has another chance to redeem a loss or failure, e.g. by winning a game or succeeding in a venture; the negative form *there is* (or *will be*) *no tomorrow* indicates that the loss or failure is final. Used in the USA since around 1960 or earlier; also used in the UK. The phrase is based on the aphorism *tomorrow is a new day* (which dates back to the 16th century or earlier), probably influenced by the famous closing words of Margaret Mitchell's novel *Gone with the Wind* (1936): 'After all, tomorrow is another day.' See also **like there was no tomorrow.**

there must be an easier way (or **easier ways**) **of making a living** applied to any difficult, dangerous, arduous or exasperating occupation;

also used jocularly at a time when the speaker's occupation seems particularly difficult, arduous, etc., as in *I'm taking 40 ten-year-olds on a school trip to the zoo tomorrow – there must be easier ways of making a living!* Since the mid-1940s. The phrase occurs in Brian Lecomber's thriller *Turn Killer* (1975), where a stunt flyer records: 'I was ... listening to a still small voice somewhere in my head, saying for the thousandth time that there must be an easier way of making a living.'

there ought to be a law against it! an expression of disgust; also used jocularly or ironically. Since around 1960 or earlier. It may be derived from the phrase *there ought to be a law,* which formed the title of a syndicated comic strip by the US newspaper cartoonist Jimmy Hatto in the 1940s–50s.

there's a nigger in the woodpile there is something wrong or suspicious (about a situation or person). Used in the USA since the mid-19th century; also used in the UK. The phrase *nigger in the woodpile* is applied to a hidden catch, snag, hindrance or other cause of trouble; it also occurs in such constructions as in *he* (or *she*) *is* (or *was*) *the nigger in the woodpile,* applied to the person on whom suspicion rests, or who is responsible for what has gone wrong. The occasional variant *there's a nigger in the woodshed* may have been influenced by **he** (or **she**) **has seen something nasty in the woodshed**.

there's gold in them thar hills applied to an enterprise that is (likely to be) highly lucrative; also used ironically, impugning the probability of some extravagant hope. The phrase probably originated in the days of the great US gold rush of the mid-19th century and is chiefly associated with Western films depicting that era; it was adopted as a catch phrase in the UK during the 1930s. A cartoon in the *Sunday Telegraph* (7 April 1974) featured two miners looking at a couple of great slagheaps (an allusion to a land-deal scandal concerning reclaimed land), with the caption: 'I'm telling you – there's gold in them thar hills.'

there's life in the old dog yet he is still very much alive, still capable of love, sex, etc.; said of or by one who might be considered 'past it'. Possibly since the mid-19th century. The phrase occurs in H. V. Esmond's play *The Law Divine* (1918): '"He's much too old to go messing about with widows." "There's life in the old dog yet."' A feminine variant, with *girl* in place of *dog,* was used by Noël Coward as the title of a dramatic sketch (written in 1923).

there's no answer to that! a response to any appropriate remark, especially one that can be interpreted with sexual innuendo. It was a catch phrase of the comedian Eric Morecambe, who used it from the late 1960s in response to such remarks as 'I have a long felt want.'

there's no harm in trying see **no harm in trying**.

there's no rest for the wicked! see **no rest for the wicked!**.

there's no two ways about it it is so, and not otherwise. The phrase emphatically affirms the truth or validity of the following or preceding statement, as in *he's a good-for-nothing layabout – there's no two ways about it*. Used in the USA since the mid-19th century and in the UK in the 20th century. A more grammatical variant is *there are no two ways about it*.

there's nowt so queer as folk a comment upon (an example of) human unpredictability, eccentricity, oddity, nonconformity, etc. The phrase originated in Yorkshire in the mid-19th century and has been widely used in other parts of the country since around 1890.

there's one born every minute refers to somebody who is particularly gullible or easily duped, or to such people in general (with the implication that there are many of them); often used by those who exploit the gullible or, ruefully, by one who has been duped. A catch phrase of the 20th century, it is elliptical for the saying 'There's a sucker born every minute', attributed to the 19th-century circus magnate P. T. Barnum.

there's (plenty) more where that came from a catch phrase of the radio series *The Goon Show* (first broadcast in 1952), where it was most frequently heard in the form *and there's more where that came from*.

there's safety in numbers see **safety in numbers**.

there's trouble at t'mill see **trouble at t'mill**.

they charge like the Light Brigade (or **a wounded bull**) see **charge like the Light Brigade**.

they don't yell, they don't tell, and they're very (very) grateful a young man's tribute to older women and their alleged response to amorous or sexual advances. The phrase has been in general use since around 1920, although the observation on gratitude was adumbrated in an essay by Benjamin Franklin, written in the mid-18th century, on choosing a mistress. A variant is *they don't yell, they don't tell, they don't swell, and they're grateful as hell*.

they fit where they touch see **it fits where it touches**.

they think their shit doesn't stink applied to conceited or would-be superior people; also used in the singular form *he* (or *she*) *thinks his* (or *her*) *shit doesn't stink*. Since around 1870.

they went thataway see **went thataway, he** (or **they**).

they're two (or **ten**) **a penny** they are easy to come by, so numerous that they are expendable or hardly worth notice, etc., as in *good secretaries are not two* (or *ten*) *a penny, you know*. The phrase probably dates from the late 19th century. It occurs in the New English Bible

(Matthew 10:29): 'Are not sparrows two a penny?', though these words of Jesus are better known in the form of the corresponding quotation from the Authorized Version: 'Are not two sparrows sold for a farthing?'

thick as two short planks(, as)   extremely stupid. Probably since the mid-20th century or earlier. Variants include *(as) thick as a plank*, *(as) thick as a short plank*, and *(as) thick as a four-inch plank*.

things ain't what they used to be   see **fings ain't wot they used t'be**.

things I do for you!, the   said with a jocular or ironic air of martyrdom by one performing a difficult, menial, unpleasant, or otherwise undesirable task for another. It dates from around 1955 as an established catch phrase.

think nothing of it!   you're welcome; that's all right; a conventional polite response to an expression of gratitude, apology, etc., as in *'Thanks for your help.' 'Think nothing of it.'*; *'I'm sorry to have kept you waiting.' 'Think nothing of it!'* Since the 1940s.

thinks his (or **her**) **shit doesn't stink, he** (or **she**)   see **they think their shit doesn't stink**.

thinks the sun shines out of (sb's) arsehole, he (or **she**)   he (or she) idolizes or greatly admires the specified person (e.g. a member of the opposite sex; a favourite child, pupil, employee, etc.; or even oneself); often used disparagingly. Late 19th–20th centuries (but perhaps of much earlier origin). The word *arsehole* may be replaced by other synonyms, notably *arse* or *backside*, as in Julian Symons' *A Three Pipe Problem* (1975): 'And you said yourself that those two old people thought the sun shone out of Gledson's backside.'

this hurts me more than it hurts you   see **this will hurt me more than it hurts you**.

***this* I *must* hear** (or **see**)!   an expression of amused or ironic incredulity, as in *'I've got a good excuse.' 'This I must hear.'* The phrase may have originated in the USA in the 1930s as the punch-line of a Yiddish joke: 'Couple in a honeymoon bedroom: "I'll get on top." "No, I'll get on top." "No, let's both get on top." Eavesdropper: *"This I must see."* (The couple are trying to close a suitcase.)'

this is a bit of all right!   this is excellent, very cosy, very welcome, etc. A chiefly Cockney catch phrase of the 20th century. It is an extension of the slang phrase *a bit of all right*, which is also applied to an attractive and/or compliant female.

this is going to hurt me more than it hurts you   see **this will hurt me more than it hurts you**.

this is so sudden!   a jocular or ironic response to an unexpected offer or gift. Since the 19th century or earlier. The phrase is also used when somebody accidentally touches a person of the opposite sex in a way that could be interpreted as an amorous or sexual advance; this modern usage probably dates from around 1950. See also **I didn't know you cared.**

this is something like! an expression of enthusiastic approbation. The phrase dates from the 17th century or earlier; it occurs in Richard Brome's comedy *The Covent Garden Weekend* (published in 1658): 'This is something like! These appear like Buildings! Here's Architecture exprest indeed! It is a most sightly situation and fit for Gentry and Nobility.'

this is the end! this is intolerable or outrageous. The phrase may have originated around the outbreak of World War I in 1914.

this is the life! said by one enjoying a situation of great comfort, luxury, indulgence, pleasure, etc., especially temporarily (e.g. on holiday). Since around 1910; also used ironically by soldiers during World War I.

this is where the men are separated from the boys see **separate the men from the boys, that'll** (or **this'll**).

this is where we came in we've seen or heard all this before (so it's time we stopped, departed, etc.); used e.g. when an argument or discussion comes full circle, or when a situation begins to repeat itself. A catch phrase that dates from the 1920s. It originated, of course, in the days of continuous showings at the cinema: those who 'came in' after the film had begun could stay on at the end to watch the part they had missed.

this is your captain speaking a jocular or mock-pompous declaration made by one who has assumed control of any situation, however trivial. Since around 1965 or earlier. From the introductory statement made by the captain of a passenger plane or ship.

this week's deliberate mistake applied to any unwitting error after it has been brought to the attention of its perpetrator, as in *'You've missed the 'r' out of 'February'.' 'Well done – you've spotted this week's deliberate mistake!'* The phrase originated in the 1930s, during a programme in the radio series *Monday Night at Seven*: the presenter made a glaring but unintentional error, listeners phoned in to correct him, and the broadcast ended with a face-saving remark along the lines of 'I wonder how many of you spotted my deliberate mistake?' It was subsequently decided to keep *this week's deliberate mistake* as a regular feature of the series.

this will hurt me more than it hurts you said, for example, by a parent or teacher about to administer corporal punishment to a child. This cliché – usually a barefaced lie – has become a derisive catch phrase applied to any similar excuse for punishment, rejection, disappointment, etc. Since around 1920. Variants of the phrase have *this hurts me* or *this is going to hurt me* in place of *this will hurt me.*

this won't buy (the) baby a frock   this won't do!; said by or to somebody who is idle, wasting time, resting, etc. A catch phrase of the 20th century, used with increasing rarity in the UK since around 1940. Variants have *a new dress* (or *bonnet*) or *a new pair of shoes* (or *boots*) in place of *a frock.*

though I says it as shouldn't   see **although** (or **though**) **I says it as shouldn't.**

thought you'd never ask! (**, I**)   a jocular response to a long-expected or hoped-for invitation (such as 'How about a drink?') or other query (such as 'How did you get on?'). It achieved catch-phrase status in the later 20th century.

throws money around like a man with no arms   see **he flings** (or **throws**) **money around like a man with no arms.**

till death us do (or **do us**) **part**   applied jocularly to marriage, or ruefully to any irksome responsibility or undesirable situation from which one can never hope to escape (e.g. a burdensome dependant, an unwelcome public office, an addiction to drugs or alcohol, etc.). The phrase is, of course, derived from the marriage service in the *Book of Common Prayer*; it was popularized in the UK as the title of a television comedy series (first broadcast in 1964), featuring Warren Mitchell as the loud-mouthed Alf Garnett and Dandy Nichols as his long-suffering wife.

till hell freezes over   for ever; used as a letter-ending and also in speech, often ironically, as in *you'll have to wait till hell freezes over for them to admit they've made a mistake.* It probably originated in the USA in the late 19th century and was subsequently adopted in the UK. The related phrase *when hell freezes over* means 'never'.

time, gentlemen, please: haven't any of you got a home to go to?   heard in public-houses when customers are unwilling to depart. Since around 1925. The second part of the catch phrase has a number of variants, such as *ain't you got no homes to go to?*, and is sometimes used alone in other contexts, e.g. after a party.

time I wasn't here (**, it's**)   I ought to have departed before now, as in *good heavens, it's half past eight – time I wasn't here!* A catch phrase of the 20th century. Other personal pronouns may be used in place of *I*, as in *(it's) time you weren't here.*

to coin a phrase   used ironically, before or after a cliché or other idiomatic phrase, by way of excuse or apology, as in *that's right up my street, to coin a phrase, to coin a phrase, we've got them by the short and* *curlies*. Since the 1940s.

today . . ., tomorrow the world! applied (often ironically or dispara-gingly) to any project or achievement, meaning 'who knows what heights of success I (or we, you, they, etc.) may reach?' The phrase may have originated in Germany in the 1930s – in the *Bloomsbury Dictionary of Popular Phrases* Nigel Rees supplies a rough translation of the closing lines of a Hitler Youth song: 'For today Germany belongs to us / And tomorrow the whole world.' In more recent US and British usage the phrase has been associated with show business, used e.g. of a performer, act or show that has its first success at a relatively minor location (as in *today Croydon, tomorrow the world!*), and is also found in sporting or commercial contexts.

tonight's the night! indicates the imminence of something import-ant, especially the sexual culmination of an amorous liaison (to the extent that the phrase may be used with jocular sexual innuendo in other contexts). It dates from around 1913, when it was popularized at the title of a musical comedy.

too bloody Irish! too true!; an emphatic, usually rueful, expression of agreement. Since around 1870 or earlier. The phrase is probably derived from *too Irish stew*, rhyming slang for 'too true', shortened and intensified.

too many chiefs and not enough Indians see **all chiefs and no Indians.**

too too applied to any instance of excess. The phrase became popular with fashionable society in the early 1880s. An example of it can be traced back to *Our Mutual Friend* (1865) by Charles Dickens: 'A too, too smiling large man, with a fatal freshness on him'; (Chapter 2). It is used adverbially in Evelyn Waugh's *Vile Bodies* (1930): 'How devastating, how un-policemanlike, how goat-like, how sick-making, how too, too awful.' See also **not quite quite.**

touch wood! a superstitious cliché used jocularly as a catch phrase; uttered to avert bad luck or a reversal of the good luck of which one has just boasted, as in *I've never had a car accident, touch wood!* It is traditionally accompanied by the act of touching something wooden (or, jocularly, one's own or another's head, to which a stock rejoin-der is *wood from the tree of knowledge!*). The origin of the superstition is uncertain: the phrase may allude to the wood of the cross on which Christ was crucified (or supposed splinters of this sold as relics), or to a pagan tradition involving the worship of trees or forest deities. The full form of the saying is *touch wood, it's sure to come good*; the US equivalent is *knock on wood!*

tough act to follow see **act to follow, a hard** (or **tough**).

tough shit! bad luck!; usually indicates a total lack of interest in and/or sympathy with the problems of the person addressed. Of US origin, the phrase probably became more widespread during World War II. Like **tough titty!**, it is often shortened to *tough!* See also **hard cheese!**

tough titty! bad luck!; often used ironically, as an expression of utter indifference to the misfortunes or unhappiness of others. The phrase may have originated in the USA in the 1920s. From *titty*, meaning 'teat; nipple'; perhaps a shortening of the phrase *tough titty breaks the baby's teeth*. See also **hard cheese!**; **tough shit!**

trouble at t'mill(, **there's**) (usually said in a mock Yorkshire or Lancashire accent) a cliché of stories and dramas of the 19th–20th centuries, referring to the inevitable confrontation between wicked mill-owner and restive workers; used jocularly as a catch phrase in any appropriate situation (not necessarily involving industrial relations). The phrase was satirized in the television series *Monty Python's Flying Circus*, at the beginning of the famous 'Spanish Inquisition' sketch (first broadcast in 1970): 'Mr Wentworth just told me to come in here and say there was trouble at the mill, that's all. I didn't expect a kind of Spanish Inquisition.'

try it on the dog!(, **let's**) let's experiment safely. Since around 1890; of theatrical origin.

try this for size! accompanies a (usually playful) punch; also used when offering a drink, book, etc., meaning 'see whether you like this' or 'will this do?' Since around 1930. The phrase originated in the jargon of those selling hats, shoes or other items of personal attire.

TTFN see **ta-ta for now!**

twisting slowly, slowly in the wind a catch phrase of US political origin. According to William Safire (in 'Political Word Watch', *The New York Times*, 19 November 1978), the phrase is 'likely to be used whenever Presidents let their nominees go without support'. It may have been coined by John Ehrlichman (one of Richard Nixon's aides), who remarked in March 1973 of Patrick Gray (nominee for the post of Director of the FBI): 'I think we ought to let him hang there. Let him twist slowly, slowly in the wind.'

two a penny see **they're two** (or **ten**) **a penny**.

two cents' worth one's opinion or advice, for what it's worth, especially in *to put in one's two cents' worth*. The phrase is also loosely applied to any idle remark or unsought comment, as in *who asked you to put in your two cents' worth?* Used in the USA since the early 1940s; also used in the UK.

U

unaccustomed as I am to public speaking   used jocularly by way of introduction to a speech, especially ironically or quasi-apologetically by one suffering from no such handicap. Since around 1950.

unhand me, villain (or **sir**)!   a cliché of 19th–20th century melodrama, used jocularly as a catch phrase in any appropriate context. The phrase sometimes means no more than 'go away!' or 'stop bothering me!'

up Alice's   a jocular reply to such questions as 'Where did you get to last night?' or 'Where are you going this evening?' The phrase probably originated in the North Country in the late 19th or early 20th century. The allusion is, of course, sexual – a pun on the literal sense of 'up at (or to) Alice's house'.

up and down like a bride's nightie   applied to somebody who is very restless or frequently disturbed. Since the mid-1930s. The phrase has numerous variants, used in this or other senses (e.g. applied to somebody repeatedly promoted and demoted, or to the ups and downs of fortune). These include *up and down like a yo-yo, . . . like a whore's drawers on Boat Race night, . . . like a fiddler's elbow* and *. . . like a shithouse seat.* See also **off like a bride's nightie.**

up, Guards, and at 'em!   an expression of light-hearted or nonchalant defiance or jocular encouragement. A catch phrase of the late 19th–20th centuries, based on a probably apocryphal quotation attributed to the Duke of Wellington at the Battle of Waterloo.

up shit creek without a paddle   in a serious predicament with no discernible relief at hand. A polite variant has *the* in place of *shit*, often shortened to *up the creek.* The phrase probably originated in the USA in the early 20th century; it has been widely used in the UK since around 1945.

use your imagination   addressed, for example, to one who feigns innocence or ignorance of the matter in hand. Since the early 1940s.

V

ve haf vays of making you talk (said in a sinister mock-German accent) a cliché of films and television series featuring the Gestapo or the SS; used jocularly as a catch phrase, sometimes anglicized to *we have* . . . and/or with a different verb in place of *talk*. The mock-German form was further popularized by the US television series *Rowan and Martin's Laugh-In* (first broadcast in 1967, also in the UK). The phrase may have originated in the pre-Nazi era: the film *Lives of a Bengal Lancer* (1935) contains the line 'We have ways of making men talk', spoken by the evil Mohammed Khan.

vergin' on the ridiculous follows any mention of the word *virgin*, especially when the virginity of a girl or young woman is in question. A catch phrase of the later 20th century.

very interesting . . . but stupid! a catch phrase of the US television series *Rowan and Martin's Laugh-In* (first broadcast in 1967, also in the UK), usually spoken in a German accent by Arte Johnson, dressed as a German soldier. The phrase was used by Nigel Rees as the title of a book of catch phrases from the world of entertainment (1980).

very nice too!(, **and**) well, aren't you (or isn't he, she, etc.) lucky!, as in *'He's just come into a fortune.' 'Very nice too!'* The phrase is also used in other contexts, as an expression of admiration or approval. Since around 1920 at the latest.

vive la différence! usually refers to the difference between the sexes; as in *'Women are far more emotional than men.' 'Vive la différence!'* From a French male toast, adopted in the UK around 1920. It is also used in the context of racial or political diversity.

vote early and often a catch phrase that may have originated in the USA in the mid-19th century; now used jocularly or facetiously, rather than as incitement to ballot-rigging. Variants include *vote early, vote often* – described in *The Oxford Dictionary of Modern Quotations* as a 'Chicago (and Irish) election proverb' – and *vote early and vote often*.

W

wait and see! a catch phrase associated with the British statesman Herbert Henry Asquith, nicknamed 'Old Wait and See' after fielding questions about the Finance Bill (1910) with the non-committal reply: 'We had better wait and see.' The phrase had undoubtedly been in use for many years previously: in *The Methuen Dictionary of Clichés* Christine Ammer supplies an example from Daniel Defoe's *Robinson Crusoe* (1719).

wait for it! used, for example, by one telling a joke or recounting an amusing incident, as a build-up to the punch-line or when the audience laughs in anticipation of the punch-line. The phrase may have originated in the armed forces during World War I (from literal usage in the sense of 'wait for the word of command'), or it may be of 19th-century music-hall origin, meaning 'wait for the laughter to die down before resuming the dialogue'.

wake up and smell the coffee! stop dreaming!; you're not facing the facts. Chiefly used in the USA. If the phrase did not originate as an advertising slogan, it was possibly prompted by various aromatic advertisements for coffee.

wakey, wakey! addressed not only to those who are (or appear to be) asleep, but to anybody who is slow in moving along, getting something done, grasping the obvious, etc. The phrase was popularized by the band-leader Billy Cotton as the cheerfully strident introduction to his radio and television *Band Show* (first broadcast in 1949). It is sometimes used in combination with **rise and shine**.

wanna fight? I'll hold your coat see **hold me back!**

want to make something of it? a threatening response to criticism or insult, implying a readiness to fight. Since around 1925. A neat example occurs in John Mortimer's play *Collaborators* (1973): '"Where were you raised?" "The rough end of Godalming. Want to make something of it?"' A variant is *want to start something?*

warts and all applied e.g. to a biography that does not attempt to conceal or omit any of the faults or failings of the subject. The phrase is derived from Oliver Cromwell's instructions to the portrait painter Lely: 'Mr Lely, I desire you would use all your skill to paint my picture

truly like me, and not flatter me at all; but remark all these rough-
nesses, pimples, warts, and everything as you see me.'

was my (or **his, her,** etc.) **face red!**   see **is my face red!**

watch my dust!   said by one who intends to depart at speed. Probably
since the late 19th century. An allusion to the dust raised by the
hooves of a galloping horse. Variants of the phrase have *smoke* or
speed in place of *dust.*

watch my lips   see **read my lips.**

watch the dicky bird!   used especially when photographing children,
in the hope that they will gaze at the camera lens with bright,
expectant faces. Since the late 19th century. A frequent variant is
watch the birdie! Both phrases have been largely superseded in the
second half of the 20th century by *say cheese!* (a word that stretches
the mouth into a grin).

water under the bridge, it's (or **that's**) **all**   applied   dismissively   to
things that are over and done with, no longer worth bearing in mind,
etc., as in *she and I had a row over a boyfriend many years ago, but that's
all water under the bridge.* A catch phrase of the 20th century.

we aim to please   a jocular response e.g. to an expression of appreciation, as in *'That's very good of you.' 'We aim to please.';* also used
ironically, as in *'I like your cheek!' 'We aim to please.'* Since the 1930s.
The phrase originated in advertisements for travel agencies, department stores, etc.; as a catch phrase used by an individual the *we* is
'royal'. It gave rise to the following graffito (or sign) in men's toilets:
'We aim to please; you aim too, please.'

we all have our moments   we've all had brief periods of sexual satisfaction, success, etc. Since 1950 at the latest. An earlier sense of the
phrase, in which *moments* refers to odd ways or aberrations, dates
from around 1920. See also **I've had my moments.**

we are not alone   be quiet – I think somebody is listening or, at least,
close enough to overhear. Since around 1910; probably more common in the USA than in the UK. From literal usage of the phrase in
melodrama, etc.

we are not amused   said in a mock-regal tone of voice, in imitation of
Queen Victoria (to whom the phrase is attributed). The circumstances in which the queen used these words (if she ever uttered
them at all) are uncertain; the catch phrase is often used in response
to light-hearted mockery, a practical joke, etc.

we can't go on (or **we must stop**) **meeting like this**   see **meeting like
this, we can't go on** (or **we must stop**).

we have ways of making you talk   see **ve haf ways of making you talk.**

we speak the same language   we think and feel alike; we're on the same wavelength; we're in complete accord. Since the late 1950s or early 1960s. The phrase is also used in other persons.

we was (or **wuz**) **robbed!** used jocularly or indignantly by one who has been tricked or outsmarted. The phrase is attributed Joe Jacobs, manager of the US boxer Max Schmeling, who disputed the latter's defeat by Jack Sharkey in the 1932 heavyweight title fight; it is also used as a catch phrase in similar sporting contexts. Also *you were robbed* said to someone who has paid too much for something, or has boasted of buying a bargain that was not worth buying, in the speaker's opinion.

we're in business indicates that the first stage of any enterprise (not necessarily commercial) has been successfully accomplished. Since the 1950s.

we're just good friends our relationship is purely platonic, not amorous or sexual; a disclaimer used, for example, by those in the public eye who have become the focus of media speculation, by a couple suspected of an illicit or scandalous liaison, or by any two people who are often seen about together. Since the 1930s. The phrase is usually greeted with scepticism, and may be used jocularly by those who do not expect to be believed, especially when there is ample evidence to the contrary. The 1980s television comedy series *Just Good Friends* featured such a relationship.

we've got a right one 'ere! refers to a fool or a very odd person indeed; used as a jocular aside by comedians and other popular entertainers, including Dick Emery (in *Educating Archie*, 1950s), Tony Hancock, Frankie Howerd, and Bruce Forsyth (in *The Generation Game*, 1970s). The phrase probably originated around 1940.

wear it in health said when making a present of an article of clothing or a piece of jewellery; a Jewish conventionalism used jocularly as a Gentile catch phrase. It is also loosely applied to any gift, possession, opportunity, experience, etc., in the sense of 'enjoy whatever you get'. Possibly since the late 19th century.

welcome aboard! a greeting to a newcomer to any institution or enterprise, especially a business or other place of work. The phrase has been used in this way since the mid-1940s or earlier. It is probably of naval origin, and has also been used to welcome passengers aboard civilian aircraft.

well, I (do) declare! an exclamation of astonishment or shock. Since around 1830; now chiefly used as an ironic, self-conscious archaism. Of US origin, the phrase is often pronounced in a parody of the accent of the southern USA.

well, I like that! see **I like that!**

well, if you knows of a better 'ole(, go to it)!   see **if you knows of a better 'ole(, go to it)!**

well, what do you know!   an expression of genuine or ironic surprise, as in *'It didn't work.' 'Well, what do you know!'* Since around 1920. The word *well* is sometimes dropped (see **what do you know!**). See also **how about that!**

went down like a lead balloon, it (or **that**)   applied to anything that is spectacularly unsuccessful, e.g. a joke, a show, a plan, a suggestion, etc. Used in the USA since around 1950; also used in the UK.

went thataway, he (or **they**)   a cliché of Western films and novels, used jocularly or allusively as a catch phrase since the 1930s. The phrase is usually accompanied by an outstretched arm pointing in the direction of departure (or, misleadingly, in the opposite direction).

were you born in a barn?   addressed to one who leaves a door open, especially when this creates an undesirable draught. Since the mid-19th century or earlier. The phrase has numerous variants, including *you must have been born in a field with the gate open.*

wha' hap'?   see **what's happening?**

wham, bam, thank you, ma'am   a cynical or jocularly brutal comment on sexual intercourse, usually referring to a quick act of copulation characterized by a lack of finesse and consideration for the woman's satisfaction. The phrase has been used in the USA since around 1895 and in the UK since the early 1940s. In US slang *wham-bam* is an adverb or adjective meaning 'quick(ly) and rough(ly)'.

what a life!   applied jocularly to some trivial misfortune, humdrum task, etc., or ironically to a desirable lifestyle, as in *what a life – nothing to do all day but lie in the sun!* Since the 19th century or earlier.

what a nerve!   see **of all the nerve!**

what a shower!   refers to a worthless, contemptible, undesirable or unimpressive individual or group of people. The phrase originated in the armed forces around 1919, directed e.g. at an intake of new recruits. The word *shower* is probably elliptical for *shower of shit.*

what a turn-up for the book!   an expression of surprise (and often pleasure) at the unexpected. The phrase *a turn-up for the book,* an allusion to bookmaking, also occurs in other constructions, especially *that's a turn-up for the book!* Since the 1930s or earlier.

what a way to run a railway (or **railroad**)!   applied to a situation of more or less organized chaos. Of US or Canadian origin; subsequently adopted in the UK. The phrase was used in the 1920s or 1930s as the caption of a US cartoon featuring a signalman coolly watching two of trains collide beneath his box. A variant is *that's a hell of a way to run a railway* (or *railroad*)!

what about the workers? (usually *wot abaht . . .*, for proletarian auth-enticity) used as a catch phrase in any appropriate situation, in parody of the traditional Labour heckler's cry. Since the 1950s. It became part of a catch phrase used by Harry Secombe in the UK radio series *The Goon Show* (first broadcast in 1952): 'Hello, folks, and what about the workers?'

what can you expect from a pig but a grunt? you can't expect civility from an ill-mannered person. Late 19th–20th centuries. Prompted by the proverb *you can't make a silk purse out of a sow's ear.*

what did your last servant die of? said when one is asked to do some-thing for another, with the implication that the person addressed is too lazy to do it himself or herself. Probably since the 1890s or earlier. A variant is *when did your last servant die?*

what do you know! a shortening of **well, what do you know!**, as in *hey, what do you know – Jack's getting married at last!*; possibly the original form of the phrase.

what do you take me for? usually means 'do you think I'm a fool?' or 'what sort of a girl or woman do you think I am?'; also used in indignant response to any other implication, e.g. of dishonesty, disloyalty, etc. The phrase has been current throughout the 20th century.

what do you think that is – Scotch mist? addressed sarcastically to one who fails to see something that is clearly visible, obvious, etc. The phrase originated in the armed forces in the mid-1920s.

what do you want – jam on it? aren't you satisfied?; said to somebody who grumbles, or used ironically when the complaint is justified. Late 19th–20th centuries. The US equivalent is *what do you want – egg in your beer?* See also **d'you want jam on both sides?**

what else did you get for Christmas? addressed sarcastically to some-body showing off with a new 'toy', especially a motorist driving a car fast and/or noisily, sounding the horn, flashing the lights, etc. Since around 1965.

what else is new?(, **so**) a sarcastic response to a piece of stale news, or to something predictable, as in *'The government's done a U-turn.' 'So what else is new?'* The phrase originated in the USA, perhaps as early as 1890. See also **tell me news (– that's ancient history)!**; **tell me something I don't know!**

what gives? what's happening? Adopted from the USA around 1945; possibly of German or Yiddish origin.

what goes up must come down a truism based on the law of gravity, used in any appropriate context, e.g. as a comment upon pregnancy. Late 19th–20th centuries.

what has he (or **she**) **got that I haven't (got)?**   said of a rival, e.g. by a jilted lover. Used by one whose partner has been unfaithful during a period of separation, the phrase may be met with the down-to-earth (if insensitive) response 'nothing, but it was available'. Since the 1930s. The phrase is also used in other contexts, of anybody who seems to have more success than the speaker, who is chosen in preference to the speaker, etc.

what have you got to lose?   the proposed course of action has few or no risks, so you might as well try it; also addressed to one who has already lost everything. The phrase may occur in other persons and is variable in form, as in *what have I* (or *we*) *got to lose?*; *what can you lose?*; *what is there to lose?*; *there's nothing to lose*, etc.

what says the enemy?   see **how goes the enemy?**

what the well-dressed . . . is wearing   usually directed ironically or derisively at somebody wearing ill-fitting or scruffy clothes, fancy dress, etc.; occasionally used as a term of approbation. Any noun may be substituted for the ellipsis, e.g. *executive, schoolteacher, slob, tart*, etc. The phrase probably originated as the slogan of a tailor or couturier; it has been used as a catch phrase since the mid-20th century.

what was the name of the engine-driver?   a derisive or provocatively interrogative catch phrase, used either to express boredom or to start a discussion or argument. Variants include *what was the colour of the engine-driver's whiskers* (or *eyes* or *socks*) *?* 20th century. The phrase probably originated as the facetious response to an elaborate mathematical problem about train speeds and departure and arrival times, or as the conclusion to a spoof problem of this nature. There may also be a pun on *Watt*, the name of the famous Scottish engineer associated with the development of the steam engine.

what *will* they think of next?   an expression of jocular or ironic astonishment at some new invention, idea, etc. It has been used as a catch phrase since the late 1950s, in parody of a question often asked by the naïve.

what would happen if you were in an accident?   addressed to one whose underwear is not in perfect condition, e.g. by mother to child. Probably since the 19th century. The phrase has numerous variants, including *what if you were knocked down in the street?* and *you might get knocked down* (or *hit*) *by a bus.*

what would shock me would make a pudding crawl   I'm not easily shocked; it takes a lot to shock me. The phrase probably originated around 1880.

what you see is what you get   used with jocular irony; also flirtatiously or provocatively in sexual contexts. Since around 1920. The phrase has been given a new lease of life in computer terminology, where it is usually abbreviated to WYSIWYG and means 'what you see on the computer screen is what you get on the printout' – an exact reproduction of typeface, graphics, etc.

what does a man have to do to get a beer around here? said, for example, by a visiting friend who is not offered a drink soon after his arrival. Used in the USA since the 1930s; also used in the UK. The phrase originated in literal usage in brothels, etc.

what's a nice girl like you doing in a place like this? a conversational gambit used jocularly or self-consciously as a catch phrase. Adopted from the USA around 1950 or earlier. It may have originated as a line from a second-rate film, or as a cartoon caption. In modern usage the phrase is found in all sorts of ludicrous contexts, with absurd substitutions for *girl* and *place* and/or punning transpositions of these words.

what's (all) this in aid of? what's (all) this about?; what's the purpose of (all) this?; why are you making such a fuss, going to so much trouble, etc. Since around 1918. From collections, fund-raising activities, etc., *in aid of* a good cause.

what's bit you? what's the matter?; a question prompted by curiosity rather than sympathy. The phrase dates from around 1915 or earlier. See also **what's eating you?**

what's cooking? what's happening?; what's going on here?; what's being planned? Adopted from the USA around 1940. The phrase is sometimes extended to *what's cooking, good-looking?* (with the final g's often dropped); a popular song of the late 1940s contained the line: 'Hey, good-lookin'! Whatcha got cookin'?'

what's eating you? what's annoying you? Used in the USA since around 1910; also used in the UK. Variants include *what's biting you?* and *what's bugging you?*; see also **what's bit you?**

what's happening? an informal expression of friendly greeting. The phrase is often abbreviated to *wha' hap'?*, especially in Black or dialectal usage.

what's it to you? what concern is it of yours?; mind your own business!; often said in a truculent tone of voice. Used in the USA since around 1919 and subsequently adopted in the UK. The phrase occurs in Robert Benchley's *The Questionnaire Craze*: 'The first question is a simple one. "How many hours do you sleep each night, on the average?" Well, professor, that would be hard to say. I might add "and what's it to you?" but I suppose there must be some reason for wanting to know.'

what's new?   what's the news? Since World War II or earlier. Following
   the success of the film *What's New, Pussycat?* (1965) and its popular
   title song, the phrase was frequently suffixed with *pussycat* in the
   1960s-80s.

what's that when it's at home?   what's that? – I've never heard of it;
   often directed at somebody employing an erudite or technical term
   among those unlikely to know its meaning, as in the following
   quotation from Julian Symon's *The Players and the Game* (1972): "'My
   belief is . . . that this might be a case of *folie à deux.*" "And what's that
   when it's at home?'" A catch phrase of the 20th century. The variant
   who's he (or *she*) *when he's* (or *she's*) *at home?* means 'I've never heard
   of him (or her).'

what's the big idea?   (often preceded by *hey!* or a similar exclamation)
   why are you doing (or have you done) that?, as in *I hear you've handed
   in your notice – what's the big idea?*; an expression of indignant or
   petulant remonstrance, often addressed to one who has no right to
   do (or justification for doing) the thing in question. Adopted from
   the USA around 1930.

what's the damage?   what's the cost?; how much do I owe or have to
   pay?; how much is the bill?; said, for example, at the moment of
   reckoning in a restaurant, bar, etc. Since the mid-19th century.

what's the difference between a chicken?   see **because the higher the
   fewer**.

what's the dirt?   what's the scandal?; also used in the weaker sense of
   'what's the news?' The phrase dates from the early 1930s in fashionable society usage, and occurs in Evelyn Waugh's *A Handful of Dust*
   (1934). Today it is often used in the form, 'what's the dirt on . . .
   so-and-so.'

what's the drill?   see **what's the form?**

what's the form?   what's the procedure, social custom, method, etc.?;
   what's it like?; how are things? Since the early 1920s. A (chiefly
   military) variant is *what's the drill?*

what's the score?   what's the latest information? This use of the phrase
   in non-sporting contexts dates from around 1939, when RAF pilots
   adopted it in the sense of 'what's the weather like?' Of independent
   origin, probably in the late 19th century, is the use of the phrase in
   Suffolk (and possibly elsewhere) when a man or boy appears to be
   playing 'pocket-billiards', i.e. fumbling with his genitals through the
   pocket(s) of his trousers.

what's this in aid of?   see **what's (all) this in aid of?**

what's up, Doc?   a catch phrase of Bugs Bunny (in Warner Brothers
   cartoons from 1940), usually preceded by *er,* . . . and followed by the

munching of a carrot. In general usage an attempt is usually made, with more or less success, to imitate Bugs Bunny's accent and intonation. The phrase was subsequently used as the title of a zany comedy film (1972), starring Barbra Streisand and Ryan O'Neal.

what's your beef? what are you complaining about? Of US origin. From the slang use of the word *beef* in the sense of 'to complain' or 'complaint'.

what's yours is mine, and what's mine is my own a comment upon have-it-both-ways greed and selfishness; often used jocularly by or of married couples or others who have pledged to share their possessions. Late 19th–20th centuries.

whatever turns you on a comment upon the foibles, fancies, hobbies or interests of others, which do not coincide with one's own; often used jocularly, especially with sexual innuendo, as in *'I like to go to bed with a hot drink.' 'Whatever turns you on!'* The phrase dates from before the 1960s.

wheel it on! let's have it!; bring it in (or on). The phrase probably originated in the RAF in the late 1930s, entering general civilian usage in the mid-1940s. The similar phrase *wheel him in!*, meaning 'bring (or show) him in', may have originated in the army, the *wheel* being a drill manoeuvre usually necessary in the confined space of a room.

when all else fails, read the instructions! see **if all else fails, read the instructions!**

when did your last servant die? see **what did your last servant die of?**

when he says 'frog', she jumps the second person does what is demanded by the first – or else! The phrase is also used in other persons, as in *when she says 'frog', he jumps; I'm the boss around here – when I say 'frog', everybody jumps!* Mark Twain used this idea, based on a piece of folklore, in the title story of his first book, *The Celebrated Jumping Frog of Calaveras County* (1867).

when hell freezes over see **till hell freezes over**.

when push comes to shove when the situation becomes crucial; when it comes down to basics. A 20th-century catch phrase of US origin.

when the shit hits the fan see **shit hits the fan, the**.

when will the ghost walk? see **ghost walks on Friday, the**.

when you gotta go, you gotta go! used jocularly, especially when excusing oneself to go to the lavatory. The phrase may have originated as a reference to mortality, in US gangster films of the 1930s or (in British usage) during World War II. See also **man's gotta do what a man's gotta do, a**.

when you were just a gleam in your father's eye before you were born, as in *I was doing that when you were just a gleam in your father's eye*. The phrase dates from the 1920s or earlier. The word *gleam* may be replaced by *twinkle* or (less frequently) *glint*, and the phrase is adaptable, as in *I've known her since she was just a twinkle in her father's eye, you were only a twinkle in your father's eye at the time*, etc.

when you were wearing short pants when you were still a boy. Since around 1920. An intensive variant is *when you were wearing three-cornered pants* (an allusion to the traditional nappy), meaning 'when you were still a baby'.

when you've *quite* finished see **have you *quite* finished?**

when you've seen one, you've seen 'em all used as a cliché in a variety of contexts, usually expressing lack of interest in the object in question, and as a jocular or derisive catch phrase with reference to the male or female genitalia, meaning 'they are all the same, so yours doesn't interest or impress me'. 20th century. A variant is *when you've seen one, you've seen the lot.*

where have you been all my life? an expression of exaggerated flattery from male to female (or vice versa); often jocular or ironic. Used in the USA since the 1920s and in the UK from around 1942.

where the nuts come from said when Brazil is mentioned. This stock rejoinder was probably inspired (and certainly popularized) by a line from Brandon Thomas's farce *Charley's Aunt* (first performed in 1893): 'I'm Charley's aunt from Brazil – where the nuts come from.'

where's he (or **she**) **coming from?** a catch phrase that has evolved from the slang phrase *where (one) is coming from*, meaning '(one's) viewpoint or ego state', as outlined in *Encounter* (July 1978): 'The latest cool expression for "I understand" . . . is "I know where you're coming from".' It originated in the USA in the mid-1970s.

where's the beef? a US advertising slogan that developed into a political catch phrase. The advertising campaign (launched in January 1984) was for Wendy's Hamburgers (referring to a rival product with a big bun but little meat); the phrase was subsequently used in the US presidential campaign of the same year, notably by Walter Mondale in a televised debate with Gary Hart: 'When I hear your new ideas I'm reminded of that ad, "Where's the beef?"'

where's the fire? addressed to somebody in a hurry, especially by one who considers such haste to be unseemly or unnecessary (or even illegal, as in the sardonic use of the phrase by a police officer to a speeding motorist). Since around 1930. The phrase occurs in Hartley Howard's *Room 37* (1970): 'He did it as if he had no time to waste. I said, "Where's the fire?" "Fire, sir?" "You know darn well what

I mean . . .. Anyway, what's all the rush?'"

which would you rather, or go fishing?   see **because the higher the fewer**.

white man speak with forked tongue   a cliché of old Western films, usually said by American Indians of double-crossing white incomers; now used as a catch phrase among Whites themselves, with reference to chicanery.

who am I to contradict him (or **her**)?   a jocular expression of mock-modesty, following praise of the speaker, as in *he says I'm a genius, and who am I to contradict him?* Since around 1945.

who are these guys?   a catch phrase of the film *Butch Cassidy and the Sundance Kid* (1969), in which it is used repeatedly by the heroes with reference to a band of pursuers whom they seem unable to shake off. The phrase was rapidly taken up by young people, especially in the USA, but had largely died out by the end the 1970s.

who kicked your kennel?   see **who rattled your cage?**

who looks at the mantelpiece when poking the fire?   said by a man in response to an adverse comment about a woman's face. A variant is *you don't look at the mantelpiece when you're poking the fire.*

who needs it?   I neither need nor want it (with the implication that nobody needs or wants it). The phrase also occurs in the plural, as in *parents! Who needs them?* (the exasperated cry of a teenager). Used in the USA since around 1950 and subsequently adopted in the UK.

who rattled your cage?   means 'what's bothering you?' (see also **that really rattled his** (or **her**) **cage**) or 'who asked you to interfere?' In the second sense the phrase has the variants *who kicked your kennel?* and *who pulled your chain?*, which date from the early 20th century.

who's a pretty boy then?   a conventional form of address to a parrot or other cage-bird; jocularly misapplied (e.g. to people) as a catch phrase.

who's afraid of the big bad wolf?   an expression of defiance. It derives from a popular song written for Walt Disney's *Three Little Pigs* (1933), probably by Frank Churchill in collaboration with Ann Ronell. The phrase was subsequently adapted by Edward Albee as the title of his play *Who's Afraid of Virginia Woolf?* (1962).

who's counting?   usually refers to food or drink, as in *'Have another cake.' 'I mustn't – I've already had three.' 'Who's counting?'* (or *'You've had four, actually, but who's counting?'*). A catch phrase of Jewish origin; probably since the late 19th century.

who's for tennis?   see **anyone for tennis?**

who's he (or **she**) **when he's** (or **she's**) **at home?**   see **what's that when it's at home?**

who's minding the shop (or **store**)? who is actually in charge of this project or operation?; also used in politics, business, etc., when all those in authority appear to be absent or elsewhere. Since the 1930s. There is a joke about a dying Jew whose entire family gathers around his deathbed: he calls to each in turn, saying 'Reuben, are you there?', etc., and all reassure him of their presence, leading up to the punch-line 'So who's minding the shop?'

who's 'she' the cat's mother? see **'she' is the cat's mother** (or **grandmother**)

who's (that) taking my name in vain? said by one who hears his or her name mentioned, often (but not necessarily) in a disrespectful manner, as in *Joe to Fred: 'Don't blame me – it's all Bill's fault.' Bill: 'Who's that taking my name in vain?'* The phrase has been used in this way since the late 17th or early 18th century. From the Bible (Exodus 20:7): 'Thou shalt not take the name of the Lord thy God in vain' (one of the Ten Commandments).

who's up who (and who's paying the rent)? just what is happening?; who's in control?; applied to a state of confusion. Chiefly used in Australia; since around 1945.

whole new ball game, it's a see **ball game, it's a different** (or **whole new**).

why don't you drop dead! see **drop dead!**

why is a mouse when it spins? see **because the higher the fewer**.

wind changes you'll get stuck like that, if the see **if the wind changes, you'll get stuck like that**.

wish you were here see **having a wonderful time – wish you were here**.

with bells on means 'and *how!*'; used to add force or emphasis. Since around 1880. The phrase occurs in Agatha Christie's *Nemesis* (1971): 'How sad and tragic and terrible it all was. "'With bells on,' as you might say," said Miss Marple, using a phrase of her youth.' The bells alluded to may be those of a court jester or those on the harness of a horse. See also **it's got bells on; with knobs on**.

with brass fittings see **same to you with (brass) knobs on!, the; with knobs on**.

with difficulty! an oblique and usually jocular (but often correct) answer to questions beginning with *how*, such as 'How do I get from here to the other side of Birmingham?' or 'How *did* you get into those jeans?' Since the 1970s or 1980s.

with friends like that, who needs enemies? a comment upon some act of unhelpfulness, selfishness, betrayal, etc., by a so-called friend; also said when a friend makes a disparaging or uncomplimentary remark. Used in the USA since around 1920 and in the UK in the later 20th century.

with knobs on used both adjectivally and adverbially to add force or emphasis, as in *I'll be there with knobs on*. Late 19th–20th centuries. The variant *with brass fittings* has been used in the USA since before 1930. See also **same to you with (brass) knobs on!, the**; **with bells on**.

with me? (or **you!**) see **are you with me?**

with thumb in bum and mind in neutral see **there he stood with his finger in his ass**.

wogs begin at Calais represents the attitude of the insular Briton to foreigners of any colour. Since the 1950s. The parochial Englishman or -woman would contract the circle even further, with such variants as *wogs begin west of Offa's Dyke, . . . north of Hadrian's Wall*, etc.

women and children first! used jocularly as a catch phrase when there is no emergency; also used jocularly by men when it is not desirable to be first (e.g. embarking on a hazardous venture) or by women when it *is* (e.g. at a buffet meal). Since around 1914. (The traditional usage of the phrase, when evacuating a sinking ship, etc., dates from the mid-19th century.)

word in your shell-like, a a word in your ear (*shell-like* is elliptical for the poetic phrase *shell-like ear*), as in *may I have a word in your shell-like?* Since the mid-20th century or earlier.

words fail me I am speechless with astonishment, shock, anger, etc.; I cannot find words (or words are inadequate) to express my response (e.g. to the stupidity of others). A cliché that has achieved catch-phrase status since the 1960s.

work is the curse of the drinking classes a pun on the cliché *drink is the curse of the working classes* (which Partridge believes to have been untrue since World War II and grossly exaggerated since World War I). The punning catch phrase probably dates from the mid-1940s.

worse things happen at sea said consolingly to or resignedly by one who has suffered some relatively minor misfortune, setback, disappointment, etc. Since around 1840.

would you believe a meaningless prefix or suffix to any statement, usually expressing outrage, exasperation, etc., as in *when the cheque finally arrived it was for the wrong amount, would you believe!*; *when did he tell me he'd invited them round for dinner? Would you believe – half an hour before they were due to arrive!* The phrase may have originated on a US television show in the 1960s.

would you buy a used (or **second-hand**) **car from this man?** applied jocularly to the photograph of any man (or to the man himself), with the implication that he looks dishonest, untrustworthy, etc. The phrase probably originated in the USA in 1950s; it was popularized as the caption of a poster bearing the photograph of Richard Nixon, used (unsuccessfully) by his opponents in the 1968 presidential campaign.

wrong business, I'm (or **we're, you're,** etc.) **in the**   see   **in   the   wrong business, I'm** (or **we're, you're,** etc.).

X

X marks the spot applied as a catch phrase to trivialities, e.g. one's room in a hotel marked with a cross on a postcard. Since around 1925. In the original literal usage of the phrase, 'X' marked, for example, the place of a murder on photographs of the scene of the crime, the location of buried treasure on the map of an island, etc.

Y

ye gods and little fishes! an exclamation of contempt or amused surprise. The phrase dates back to the 1880s or earlier.

yer blood's worth bottling indicates either very warm approval or hearty congratulations. A catch phrase of Australian origin, dating from around 1950.

yes sir, no sir, three bags full, sir applied to an over-obsequious person; also used jocularly or disrespectfully by one who is ordered around by another. Since around 1910. The phrase is, of course, derived from the nursery rhyme 'Baa, Baa, Black Sheep'.

yes, we have no bananas a catch phrase that originated in the USA, in a popular song of the same name by Frank Silver and Irving Cohn (1923): 'Yes, we have no bananas, / We have no bananas today.' It was instantly taken up by the general public on both sides of the Atlantic, and was revived in the UK during the food shortage of 1940–6.

you ain't 'arf a one! addressed to somebody who is very odd or droll, or of a quirkish humour that elicits gentle mockery. From around 1890. See also **you are a one!**

you ain't heard (or **seen**) **nothin' yet!** there are even better or more impressive things to come; there are even worse or more shocking things to come. The origin of the *heard* version is attributed to the US entertainer Al Jolson, who uttered this historic line in the first full-length talking film, *The Jazz Singer* (1927), having coined the phrase some 20 years earlier (according to Martin Abramson's *Real Story of Al Jolson* (1950), cited in *The Oxford Dictionary of Modern Quotations*). The US president Ronald Reagan repopularized the *seen* version in his campaign for re-election in 1984.

you and me both! an expression of sympathetic agreement, as in *'I'm fed up with this.' 'You and me both!'* Used in the USA from the 1920s and in the UK since the mid-20th century. See also **that makes two of us**.

you and whose army? an expression of derisive defiance, addressed, for example, to one who makes a threat of aggression, as in *'I could fight you any day.' 'Oh yeah, you and whose army?'* Since around 1944.

An earlier variant is *you and who else?*

you are a one! you are droll! Probably since around 1880; mainly Cockney. In modern usage it is often said in an affected or mockingly imitative manner. See also **aren't you the one!; you ain't 'arf a one!**

you are awful(, but I like you)! (**, ooh,**) said in jocular remonstrance, usually with sexual innuendo, in any appropriate situation. It was a catch phrase of one of the female characters played by Dick Emery in his television comedy shows of the 1970s, usually delivered in response to a double entendre or risqué suggestion and traditionally followed by a hefty push or swipe of the handbag at 'her' interlocutor.

you are Mr Lobby Lud a nonsensical salutation. The phrase originated in a publicity stunt launched by the *Westminster Gazette* on 1 August 1927: a mystery man called Lobby Lud was 'on the run', and any reader who spotted him and challenged him with these words could claim the 'reward' of £50.

you beaut! an expression of warm approval or profound admiration; also used in ironic derision. The phrase originated in Australia, probably between 1910 and 1925.

you bet your life! you may be sure; certainly. Used in the USA since the 1860s and in the UK from the late 1880s. There are numerous variants, including *you bet!, you betcha!* and *you bet your sweet life!*; the US television series *Rowan and Martin's Laugh-In* (first broadcast in 1967, also in the UK) produced the ephemeral *you bet your sweet bippy!*

you better believe it! used for emphatic affirmation, often with the nuance 'it is in your interest to believe or accept it'. Used in the USA since around 1940 or earlier. The more grammatical form *you'd better believe it!* is less frequent. See also **believe you me!**

you can go off (some) people, you know jocularly addressed to somebody who has just said or done something to upset the speaker. Since around 1960.

you can put (or **shove**) **it where the monkey put** (or **shoved**) **the nuts** see **put it where the monkey put the nuts**.

you can say that again! an expression of heartfelt agreement, as in *'You must be glad it's all over.' 'You can say that again!'* Adopted from the USA in the late 1920s. It is the sort of phrase that invites facetious literal interpretation, as in a piece by John Lardner, reprinted from *Newsweek* in *Strong Cigars and Lovely Women* (1951): 'This year's drought has got real significance, and don't tell me that I can say that again. I know I can. It has got real significance.'

you can spray that again! see **spray it again, will you?**

you can talk! see **look who's talking!**

you can't take him (or **her**) **anywhere!** said when a companion embarrasses one by doing or saying something contrary to the accepted custom or social code. Since around 1945 or earlier. See also **excuse my pig: he's a friend!**; **is he with you? . . ..**

you can't take it with you   used as an excuse or justification for spending money, especially extravagantly; often addressed to one who is missing out on the pleasures of life by saving money. Perhaps since the mid-19th century. The phrase was popularized as the title of a comedy (1936) by George S. Kaufman and Moss Hart. It may have originated as a vulgarization of a phrase from the Bible (I Timothy 6:7): 'For we brought nothing into this world, and it is certain we can carry nothing out.'

you can't think!   you couldn't possibly imagine it; you'd never believe it. This usage of the phrase dates from around 1770 or earlier; it occurs in Frederick Pilon's *He Would Be a Soldier* (1776): 'Suppose you and I go this evening to Bagnigge Wells, and drink tea – the hot rolls are so nice there, you can't think!'

you can't win!   expresses the impossibility of coming out on top, or of satisfying or pleasing people, as in *if you say yes they think you're a soft touch, and if you say no they think you're mean – you can't win!* Adopted from the USA by 1960 at the latest.

you can't win 'em all!   a philosophical acceptance of defeat, failure, rejection, disappointment, etc., as in *I asked her out, and she told me to get lost – ah well, you can't win 'em all!* Used in the USA since around 1940 and the UK from around 1955. The phrase probably originated in gambling or sport. Variants include *you win some, you lose some*, which may date from the 1920s, and *you win a few, you lose a few.*

you could have fooled me   an ironic expression of scepticism or disbelief, as in *'I didn't do it on purpose.' 'You could have fooled me.'* Since around 1955.

you come home with your knickers torn and say you found the money!   see **come home with your knickers torn and say you found the money!**

you could twist my arm   said jocularly by one who needs no such persuasion, as in *'Would you like a drink?' 'You could twist my arm.'* The phrase dates from the 1940s. A variant is *you've talked me into it.*

you dirty rat!   a catch phrase attributed to the US actor James Cagney, made famous by countless impressionists. Cagney claims never to have uttered these exact words in any of his films: in *Blonde Crazy* (1931) he calls somebody a 'dirty, double-crossing rat', and in *Taxi* (1932) he uses the phrase 'you dirty, yellow-bellied rat'.

you don't get many of those to the pound   refers to a particularly well-developed pair of female breasts; chiefly used among males. A catch phrase of the 20th century, probably not earlier.

you don't have to be mad to work here, but it helps usually printed on a joke sign, displayed in offices and other places of work. Since around 1960. See also **difficult we do at once . . ..**

you don't say! an exclamation of astonishment or incredulity; often used ironically, e.g. in response to a statement of the obvious, as in *'It's raining.' 'You don't say!'* Since the late 19th century.

you don't shit on your own doorstep see **don't shit on your own doorstep**.

you haven't got the brains you were born with! usually directed in derision or exasperation at an exceptionally stupid person. A catch phrase of the 20th century.

you heard! said to one who pretends not to have heard or understood. The phrase occurs in John Osborne's *A Sense of Detachment* (1972): '"You would, you filthy old woman." "What did you say?" "You heard!"' It may be a shortening of a phrase that dates from the early 20th century, or it may have been adopted from the USA in the mid-1940s.

you hum it and I'll pick up the tune see **no, but you hum it and I'll pick up the tune**.

you kill me! you're very funny!; often used ironically. Adopted from the USA in the mid-1930s. A variant (since the early 1940s) is *you slay me!*

you know what? see **do you know what?**

you know what you can do with it I don't want it; an expression of rejection, refusal, etc., with the usual anatomically fundamental nuance (see **if you don't like it you can lump it!**; **put it where the monkey put the nuts**). Probably since the beginning of the 20th century or earlier. The phrase is also used in other persons, as in *they know what they can do with their proposal!*

you look good enough to eat you look beautiful; chiefly addressed by males to attractive females. Late 19th–20th centuries. See also **I could eat that without salt**.

you must be joking! see **you're joking!**

you must be out of your cotton-picking (or **tiny**) **mind!** said to one who makes a ludicrous statement, suggestion, proposal, request, etc. Used in the USA from around 1945 or earlier and subsequently adopted in the UK.

you must think I'm made of money! see **do you think I'm made of money?**

you name it, we have it we can supply anything you need or do anything you want done. Since the late 1940s. From literal usage of the phrase by a firm that claims to stock everything.

you need eyes in your backside! you need to be wide awake, alert, vigilant, etc.; a vulgarization of the phrase *you need eyes in the back of your head.* 20th century.

you need your head examined! you must be out of your mind! The phrase probably dates from the 1890s, when phrenology became fashionable. It is also used in other persons, as in the (probably apocryphal) Goldwynism: 'Anyone who goes to a psychiatrist needs his head examined.'

you never know your luck you might be lucky; often used optimistically or ironically when such good fortune seems unlikely. A catch phrase of the 20th century.

you pays your money and you takes your choice refers to the element of luck or risk in choosing, making a decision, etc., as in the following passage from the *New Scientist* (17 April 1975): 'The whole problem of the origin of comets is still very speculative . . .. In reviewing the theories, you pays your money and takes your choice.' The phrase appeared in *Punch* in 1846 and also occurred in a 19th-century peepshow rhyme. From literal usage by costermongers, etc.

you play the cards you're dealt you do the best you can with what you have – physically and mentally, socially and financially. Used in the USA (especially in Western films) since around 1910; also used in the UK.

you said a mouthful! you have said something particularly important, pertinent, apt, witty, etc. Adopted from the USA in the late 1920s or early 1930s. The *New Yorker* (26 May 1973) shows a maudlin, sombre drunk paraphrasing John Donne's 'No man is an island' and the barman admiringly commenting: 'Friend, you sure said a mouthful!' In British usage *you've* is often substituted for *you.*

you said it! an expression of emphatic agreement or affirmation, as in *'I think we've got a problem.' 'You said it!'*; also used in response to a self-deprecating remark, as in *'I'm not very good at this.' 'You said it(, I didn't)!'* The phrase originated in the USA around 1900 and was adopted in the UK around 1931. It occurs in Dodie Smith's *Bonnet over the Windmill* (1937): '"Funny – anyone can see you're potty about her, but you don't really like her, do you?" "You said it, lady."' An occasional British variant is *you've said it!*

you say the *nicest* things a conventional response to flattery, used as a catch phrase with simpering jocularity; also used ironically in reply to an uncomplimentary remark. Perhaps since around 1930. The phrase occurs in Hartley Howard's *Nice Day for a Funeral* (1974): '"Worried in case something might happen to me?" "Unofficially, my only worry is that something might not. Officially, I have to treat you as though you were a civilised member of society." "You say the nicest things," I said.'

you slay me! see **you kill me!**

you were just a gleam in your father's eye see **when you were just a gleam in your father's eye**.

you what? means 'what did you say?' or 'what do you mean?'; often used incredulously, derisively or aggressively, as in *'It'll cost you at least ten grand.' 'You what?'*; *'It's a question of semantics.' 'You what?'* A chiefly British catch phrase that dates from around 1950. See also **say what?**

you win some (or **a few**), **you lose some** (or **a few**) see **you can't win 'em all**.

you'd forget your head if it wasn't screwed on (properly) addressed to a very forgetful person. Since the late 19th century.

you'll be a long time dead life is short, so enjoy yourself while you can. A catch phrase of the late 19th–20th centuries. A variant is *you're a long time dead*.

you'll hate yourself in the morning see **I'll hate myself in the morning**.

you're a big girl (or **boy**) **now** addressed to teenagers or jocularly to adults in a variety of situations, meaning 'you're old enough to know the facts of life', 'you're too old for such behaviour', etc. The variant *you're getting a big girl* (or *boy*) *now* may refer to physical development. The phrase probably dates from the late 19th century. It is also used in other persons, as in *I'm a big girl* (or *boy*) *now*, an objection to the patronizing, over-protective or over-helpful attitude of others.

you're a dirty stop-out directed at one who stays out late or all night, especially habitually. The phrase is adaptable, as in *where have you been, you dirty stop-out?* A catch phrase of the 20th century.

you're a long time dead see **you'll be a long time dead**.

you're all heart! said with heavy irony to one who has been not particularly (or not at all) kind or generous. Since the 1960s. From the colloquial phrase *to be all heart*, meaning 'to be extremely kind or generous'.

you're breaking my heart see **my heart bleeds for you**.

you're damned if you do and damned if you don't you're on the horns of a dilemma. A 20th-century catch phrase that originated in the USA. Probably from the emphatic refusal *I'm damned if I do!*

you're full of shit! you're talking nonsense; you don't know what you're talking about. Probably of US origin; perhaps since around 1930.

you're getting a big girl (or **boy**) **now** see **you're a big girl** (or **boy**) **now**.

you're joking! you can't be serious; I can't believe you're serious. In

general use since around 1950 (though the existence of such a catch
phrase in the 18th century is suggested by the learned pun *you are
Josephus Rex* (i.e. Joe King), recorded in 1785). Variants include *you
must be joking!* and *you've got to be joking!* See also **are you kidding?**

you're not the only pebble on the beach   there are plenty of others, all
equally (if not more) attractive, desirable, suitable, etc.; used to
deflate the conceit or self-esteem of the person addressed. A catch
phrase that dates from the late 19th century, when it was popularized
in a song of the same name by Harry Braisted: 'If you want to win
her hand, / Let the maiden understand / That she's not the only
pebble on the beach.' See also **there are plenty more fish in the sea**.

you're so sharp you'll cut yourself   addressed to one who is particularly quick-witted, with the implication that he or she is too clever
for his or her own good. Late 19th–20th centuries. The phrase is
also used in other persons.

you're telling me!   I'm well aware of that; I agree with you wholeheart-
edly, as in *'It's not as easy as it looks.' 'You're telling me!'* Used in the USA
from the 1920s or earlier and adopted in the UK by 1933.

you're the expert   whatever you say; I'll take your word for it; after all,
you're the authority on the subject, so you should know. Since the
1930s or earlier.

you've forgotten the piano!   see **everything but the kitchen sink**.

you've got a nerve!   see **of all the nerve!**

you've got a one-track mind   addressed to one who has an excessive
interest in sex. The phrase dates from around 1920 in this sense; it
is also used in other persons and may be applied to other preoccu-
pations.

you've got another think coming   you are mistaken, as in *if that's what
you think, you've got another think coming*. The phrase is also used in
other persons, as in *if he thinks I'm going to bail him out again, he's got
another think coming*. Sometimes *thing* is heard in place of *think*,
probably mistakenly. A (chiefly US) variant, dating from the early
20th century, has *guess* in place of *think*.

you've got it made   you are (certain to be) successful; you are in an
enviably favourable position. The phrase probably originated in the
USA around 1920 and was subsequently adopted in the UK. It is also
used in other persons, as in *he's* (or *she's*) *got it made*.

you've got something there!   there is much to support what you say;
that's a good idea; you're on to something. The phrase dates from
around 1910.

you've got to be in it to win it   a synonym of the proverb 'nothing venture, nothing gain' – if you put no money into a lottery, for example,

you can't win anything. Chiefly used in Australia, since around 1950.

you've got to be joking! see **you're joking!**

you've made my day see **made my day, you've.**

you've never had it so good see **never had it so good, you've** (or **they've**, etc.).

you've talked me into it see **you could twist my arm.**

your best friend won't tell you a euphemistic reference to bad breath, body odour or any other undesirable attribute of the person addressed. The phrase probably originated (in the form *even your best friends won't tell you*) as an advertising slogan for Listerine mouthwash in the early 1920s; it was also used in advertisements for Lifebuoy soap.

your education has been sadly neglected addressed to somebody who is ignorant of or about something or other, often a matter of quite unremarkable unimportance. The phrase is usually jocular, but is occasionally said in friendly seriousness. From around 1905.

your friendly neighbourhood . . . applied to a local expert in the specified trade, profession, service, sport, etc., as in *consult your friendly neighbourhood insurance broker*. The phrase was used in (and may have originated in) a public-relations slogan of the 1960s, *your friendly neighbourhood policeman*.

your funeral, it's (or **that's**) the (usually unpleasant) consequences will be your concern, not mine, as in *if you fail your exams it's your funeral*. Since the mid-19th century. The phrase is also used in other persons, as in *'He doesn't want to take part.' 'That's his funeral.'*

your guess is as good as mine I have no more idea than you; used in response to a question to which neither party knows the answer, as in *'Where do you think she got the money from?' 'Your guess is as good as mine.'* The phrase originated in the USA around 1925 and was adopted in the UK around 1943. It occurs in C. P. Snow's *The Malcontents* (1972): '. . . he suddenly thought to ask whether they could get everything in order by Monday. . . . "Your guess is as good as mine," said Stephen.'